Surviving the Holidays

Your Guide to Reducing Stress,

Getting a Head Start and

Managing Everything during the Holidays

By
'NATIONAL SANTA™"
Tim Connaghan

Cover: Greg Gilpin, Graphic Art Center, Inc
GraphicArtCenter.com
Cover Photos: Donna Reinbold
ReinboldGallery.com

DEDICATION

This book is first and foremost dedicated to my wife, Barbara, who has, and will always be my "number one." Without her support, encouragement and perspective, I would not have had the opportunity to travel on this very special journey, and build this ministry of sorts, that brings joy to so many. I love you Barbara.

I would also like to dedicate this to all those who believe and celebrate the magic of the holiday season. Whether it be Christmas, Hanukkah, Kwanza or other winter celebrations, the world has, for centuries, looked upon this season of year as a time to give thanks; to be with and share with friends and family; and to celebrate life

Today, all corners the world celebrate something during this season. whether it be in their church or synagogue, at work or in school, or at parties or visits to friends and family, everyone celebrates the greatest joy of the season; that of giving, sharing and doing good for others.

CONTENTS

ACKNOWLEDGEMENTS

This book would not have been possible without the experience that I have had throughout my career. All that I am is a result of the path our Lord put me on so many years ago.

Who and what I am is a result of the lessons, advice, training, guidance and love that I have received over the past 70 years. I thank all who gave to me; my parents, family, teachers, employers and the many friends I have made during the past seven decades, and most importantly from my wife Barbara and daughter Morgan.

I also appreciate all that I learned in planning and logistics from my time in the Military, my volunteer work with the Jaycees, and my almost 25 years as an event planner and producer, working with the March of Dimes, American Cancer Society and other national medical associations.

I truly believe that the Lord pointed me towards the many jobs and various directions my career has taken as I know he was training me for my current life as Santa and becoming a true descendant of Saint Nicholas.

1 INTRODUCTION

Afraid you won't survive the holidays? Worried you have too much to do and are heading to a burn-out? Or are you one that possibly gets a bit depressed when the holidays arrive?

Well, I am here to let you know that you're not alone.

What if someone told you today, "There is a way to survive the Holidays." "A way to do all you want to do and not get stressed." "A way to reduce and/or eliminate the depression and stress that often accompanies the holidays."

That is what this book is about. I have pulled together some ideas, plans and examples that will help you, "Survive the Holidays."

By doing a little each month, you can reduce your December work load and reduce the Stress that comes with it. When the Holidays arrive, you'll have the satisfaction of being totally prepared and ready to truly enjoy all the Celebrations and Festivities.

If you start right now and spread out your holiday tasks over the next few months, you could possibly have a more enjoyable holiday season.

WHY SOME FOLKS SURVIVE, AND OTHERS DON'T

Tens of thousands annually stress-out during the Holidays. Even though we all have great memories and love what the Holidays bring, we sometimes try to avoid even thinking about Christmas, Hanukkah or Kwanza. In some cases, we wish it would pass quickly and be over.

So many of us stress as we worry about buying gifts, sending cards, cooking special meals or treats, and having to attend various holiday parties. No wonder they worry about surviving. No wonder they sometimes get depressed.

On the other hand, many look forward to these Holidays. They rarely stress, and most often are totally prepared for all the activities, events and tasks. These are the folks that have truly learned how to manage and enjoy the holidays.

You've seen them, the families whose homes are all decorated. Or the friends that seem to be baking and cooking all kinds of fabulous treats through the entire season. They never seem worried or stressed out.

They've totally caught up with everything, and they attend every party or social event they are invited to. These are the families that seem to get the most out of the holiday season.

But how did they do it? How did they reduce the stress? How did they by-pass depression? How were they able to do all their shopping, attend every event and do everything they wanted to do?

Very simply, they learned "How to Survive the Holidays!" Or as I like to say, "They learned how to get a head start and manage the holidays!"

Maybe you've said this or heard someone say, "Next year, I'm not waiting 'til the last minute. I'm going to plan ahead and get an early start in preparing for the Holidays."

Well, there is no better time than now, to get that jump start, and, this is very true if you're a Santa Claus like me!

I know, because I have spent the past 50 years wearing the famous red suit, and over the years "this Santa" has truly experienced the stress of a busy holiday season.

I often get so busy with visits, appearances and seeing thousands of children, that I have too little time to spend with my family and to enjoy holiday activities with friends.

And this is not what I like, or want.

From all of this, and many stories others have told me, I have learned two important things.

Most importantly, you need to do what you and your family enjoy most and not what others expect of you. It means prioritizing your commitments, simplifying your outlook and sometimes, living within your means

This also means you need to un-clutter and simplify your schedule; realize that you can't always do everything.

Secondly, you need to be more organized and plan ahead. It means a better management of your time and what you want to accomplish. It may also mean delegating some of the work and tasks to other family members and having everyone involved your Holiday plans.

I often say, "If I don't have the holiday lights on the roof and my home decorated before Thanksgiving, I am in deep trouble with the Missus!" And I might just have to spend a few nights sleeping with the reindeer!

In my early years as Santa there were a few times when the decorations never got up. Sometimes one or two strings of lights found their way up to the roof or around the windows. It was a little embarrassing for myself, and for my family. I am sure my neighbors were thinking, "if Santa can deliver millions of presents all over the world on one night, why can't he get his house decorated on time? "

Time management, and a bit of organizing, was what saved me.

With the help of some 'Efficiency Elves,' a simple plan was created that helped Mrs. Claus and I do a better job of preparing for the Holidays. This resulted in less stress for both of us and more time to enjoy our friends and family.

With a little advanced planning, spread out between now and Christmas, you too can reduce stress and have more time to enjoy the holiday season. So, as I said at the beginning of this introduction, if you start now, you can spread out your holiday tasks over the months ahead, and, by doing a little each month, you will reduce your December work load.

Won't it be great, when the Holidays arrive, to know that you are totally prepared and ready to truly enjoy all your Holiday Events and Celebrations!

2 BEGINNING STEPS

September and October are the most popular months for those who want to start planning for the holiday season. Vacations are over, the kids are heading back to school, and the daylight is slowly disappearing.

But this is also the time of year when the stress levels start to increase. The combination of work, family activities, and other obligations can quickly overload anyone's schedule.

Gloria is a good example of what normally happens. She was always busy with her husband and children. Plus she had a part time job. And, to all of that, she also had the tasks of taking care of everything around the house. She felt she did a pretty good job.

But when November arrived, she seemed to get bogged down with just too much to do and no matter how much her husband and family helped, some things always slipped through the cracks and the worry and stress of not pleasing everyone was taking a toll on her enjoyment of the Holidays.

But how do you go about reducing the stress of the holiday season? Well first, you must make the decision to do something about it. Then you need to have a plan.

This book is for Gloria and everyone else who needs to plan. It is for Mom, Dads, Grandparents, young adults and just about everyone who worries about the arrival of the holiday season.

And when you make the decision and create a plan, you will find that much of the stress and worry is diminished. Sometimes it even goes away.

YOUR WORK PREPARATIONS

Now, before you begin your planning, I would like to offer you some tips and suggestions that will make the planning much easier.

When a craftsman or tradesman gets ready for a project or task, he makes sure that he is ready. Did he budget and plan correctly? Is the working area prepped? Does he have all the necessary tools? And finally, is he fit and personally ready to go to work on the task?

So, you need to be ready. To start with, your home or work area, where you will do most of your planning, should be prepared and set up. It's important that you start by having some organizational and planning aids available in your work area and finally, you personally, need to be prepared for the task.

To begin, relax and go through this book. Some may read every page, others will just go over the table of contents, but no matter how you do it, try to know all the sections of this book and the tools and aids that it contains.

You may not read every page right now. But check out each chapter. Read the opening paragraphs and get an idea of what tools are in each chapter: in this book.

Now, take a deep breath. stretch a little and find a comfortable, well-lit place to sit. This is how you prepare to, "Get a Head Start on the Holidays!"

WHY DO OTHERS MAKE IT LOOK SO EASY?

Ever said to yourself or thought that everyone else was "Lucky," because they were not stressed during the holidays? Maybe it was because they got all their shopping and house decorating and holiday chores done early.

Well, it was not luck. There's an old saying, "Luck is being prepared when the opportunity arrives."

The task now ahead of you is to get prepared. I want to help you plan, get organized and get ready to enjoy the holiday season. Then maybe you too, will be one of those we call, "Lucky!"

The simple element of getting ahead is advanced planning. Part of this is just starting a bit early, thinking about each event or task, and reviewing what you need to do.

Part of this may also be deciding on what to eliminate. This is a part of planning that many folks forget. Sometimes the only way to reduce stress is to reduce or eliminate something.

To lighten your schedule, you may need to get rid of one or more events and tasks. Or reduce the amount of time dedicated in that area.

What can you get rid of? Is it truly necessary, or required? In making these types of decisions, you can open your calendar, or reduce the things you need to purchase or make.

WHY WE NEED TO PLAN AND SCHEDULE

Whether we are planning for the holidays, or that well-deserved summer vacation, or a major event, we often need to start months, maybe even a year earlier, and begin our planning. (think wedding, anniversary, etc.)

Have you ever planned your summer vacation in January? Maybe February? Yes, it does take a little time to plan, make reservations, etc. Well, it is the same for Christmas and the other Holidays.

This goes back to the dawn of man. Once man had an understanding of the annual change of seasons, He developed a schedule to start his planning for each season, one season ahead.

In the Spring he planned for the summer. In the Winter he planned for the Spring. In the Summer months he planned Fall and in the Fall, he looked towards the Winter months.

It is no different today. Through the centuries, this simple schedule continues. Only today, it is much more evolved and often much more complicated or busy.

Most of the tips, guides and instructions in this book can be applied to other holidays or special events, at other times of the year.

Now, some folks can plan an event or project and do all of it in their head, with nothing on paper, and I admire them. But that is not me. And, that is not most of us.

We often need to write things down, make notes, create a budget, and schedule everything. We do this because we want to keep everything organized.

When things in our lives are organized and somewhat structured, we seem more relaxed, have less worry and are more focused on our lives. So, let's get organized.

YOUR ORGANIZATIONAL TOOLS

Gloria, who I mentioned earlier, decided she needed to be more organized. So, she set about organizing; making lists, and planning her holiday schedule. All of this gave her a focus and surprisingly, many things became much clearer.

I know you want to be more organized and wish to reduce stress. Otherwise you probably would not be reading this.

So, before we get too far along, I want you to set up or collect a couple of items that will help you prepare get organized:

- A CALENDAR. This is possibly your most important tool. Here you will post dates, plus schedule times for tasks, events and activities.

- A BINDER. This will become your planning and scheduling book. Here you will keep your calendar, your check lists, lists of things to do, and your planning sheets for important tasks.

- FILE FOLDERS, or maybe an accordion file, or even large envelopes, to keep important notes, gift ideas, shopping ideas, and other items that don't fit in the binder.

A COMPUTER and/or YOUR PHONE. Most computers have ways of keeping a schedule. Likewise, many new phones have apps for keeping lists, schedules and can even send you reminders.

And there are also "clouds", and other internet platforms where you can share all your information. Plus, the internet is a great place to search for things and answers to your many questions.

HOW DO THE BASIC TOOLS HELP?

These tools, plus anything else you wish to add, will be very valuable in organizing and planning. One must be organized to get ahead and, as we go along, you will see why you need these simple items.

Knowing your schedule and what materials, resources and help you will need to finish a task or activity is part of being prepared.

Isn't it easier to do something if you know where everything is, or if you need something, where you can go to get it, or who you can ask for assistance. Knowing these simple things will ease your mind. This reduces stress and allows you to focus on the task at hand.

If you really want to know, it's just thinking ahead.

Let's make it simple here. Earlier I mentioned a carpenter or craftsman and how they prepare. But what if you are not a tradesman and you are really a homebody who sticks near home.

Have you ever prepared a dish or meal and gotten out all the utensils, ingredients and items you will need to create your little masterpiece? You don't start mixing the cake mix without having the cake pans ready. Do you?

Anytime you are even slightly prepared, a task is easier. When you are organized, you are often prepared for anything that comes your way. If there are changes, or emergencies, because you have a good plan, they are easier to handle.

It is the same with planning for the holidays. You just need to create your own plan. Decide what "you" want or need to do. Also know that sometimes planning includes knowing when to make changes.

What if you have a conflict in the calendar? What if the budget is not there? What if you cannot get the exact gift? What if the materials, ingredients or supplies are not available?

Do you cancel or throw something out or can you adjust and make changes?

Change is inevitable. There will always be those urgent requests to change something. Whether it is Mother Nature, or Mother-in Law, creating the change, something, you did not plan for, will probably happen. So, accept that fact. Know that if you have prepared yourself, you can handle anything.

❄ ❄ ❄ ❄ ❄ ❄

3 YOUR CALENDAR

Depending on what month you plan on starting, you need a calendar to set your schedule.

As we go through the month-to-month lists, there will be reminders to post important events, deadlines and reminders for working on or finishing tasks.

Subject to your personal needs, the calendar should be one that works best for you; something comfortable.

It could be those simple 8½ x 11 monthly calendar pages we used back in high school and college (is this dating me?), which you can keep in your binder, or post on a bulletin board.

Maybe you like the larger poster-sized multi-month calendars that you post on a wall or, if you are really tech-savvy, you could create a special Google Calendar, that you, and everyone in your family, can share, change and use to keep everyone updated.

Even before you start looking at a task, or some work you need to do, why not take your calendar and pencil in some of the most common events you need to be aware of or reminded of.

- Church Events

- School events, plays or pageants

- Community Events, Tree Lightings or Parades

- Annual events: Company or Family parties that are required attendance.

- Special shopping days (Black Friday etc.)

- And let's not forget the Annual Visit to Santa Claus!

I also think that everyone should make some appointments or schedule some time for themselves. You will find out more about this in the chapter titled, "Some Time for Yourself."

As you progress through your planning, you will often be referring to your calendar to schedule new items, make changes, check off things, post reminders.

That is why I suggested writing in pencil. And, it is good to periodically check the calendar to make updates and to ensure there are no conflicts.

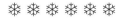

4 YOUR BINDERS AND LISTS

Not much to say here. This is just a standard binder. Maybe 1 ½" or 2" wide, where you can secure your calendar and all your to-do and check lists.

Here is what you should have in your binder:

1. Your Master Calendar. Unless this is in your computer, I recommend that you have a master calendar in your binder. This is also a great quick reference, as you are planning events or activities, and cannot access your computer immediately

2. I must admit, I have so much going on that I start with my Google calendar. But I also post on a wall calendar in my office, and sometimes create one-page planning/check lists for special trips, parties or holiday events where I have multiple things I must prepare for. The wall calendar is great for a quick "look-see" of an entire month or two in just a few seconds.

3. Checklists - You will have a variety of check lists for the holidays:

a. Christmas or Holiday Card List

b. Gift list – By name and with gift and source of gift

c. Clothing list – What are you or family members going to be wearing for parties and visits

d. Menus for those special holiday meals

e. Grocery lists – The above menus will require detailed shopping lists. This could be broken down or combined.

  Lists for canned goods, condiments, spices, and staples that have good shelf life. Lists for perishable items; produce, meats, dairy products, etc. Lists for prepared foods, pastries, cakes, etc.

f. Home decorating lists – everything from strings of lights to trees, to religious items,

g. Gift wrapping list – gift paper, tags, gift boxes, gift bags, tape, ribbon, scissors, knives, marking pens or writing pens for gift tags, etc.

h. Any other list you can think of that will make your job easier!

These lists are a starting point for you. Make them what you want. In most cases they are just simple pages in the binder where you can post some of your notes.

A collection of sample lists and forms are included in the Appendix of this book. I have also created the lists as word documents and have them available on my web site at **www.NationalSanta.com.** Just click on the tab "Surviving the Holidays."

5 YOUR FILES

As you start your planning and begin collecting notes and ideas on what you can do, or need to do, you will end up having little notes, receipts, business cards and other smaller pieces of paper that need to be saved. And they must be e saved where you can find them.

Having some file folders or possibly an accordion file, is probably the easiest way to save, and later find, these items. I really like the accordion file, as when you put something in, it will not fall out the side.

Here are some uses for your files:

- Gift ideas - Great place to save clippings or photos of items that you think would be nice gifts for select friends and family. NOTE: Although this book talks about starting in various months, I know some people who start right after the first of the year, planning for next year. They collect clippings, pages from magazines and other ideas and put them into a file. Sometimes it is just a note of a web site for a product.

- Little notes on your Christmas card list.

- Decorating ideas and new products (The various shopping networks often start promoting "Christmas in July" featuring a variety of new or popular holiday items.

- Food ideas or recipes for those special holiday meals.

- Coupons for special groceries you need to get.

- Coupons from department stores.

- Business Cards and other cards or flyers form vendors or service companies that you may need to call.

- Samples of gift wrap from last year, so you don't buy the same thing.

6 COMPUTERS, TABLETS & PHONES

This chapter is for those who are tech savvy or comfortable using new technology.

Today so many of us have some wonderful tools that we can take with us everywhere.

It's our cell phones and tablets.

With today's technology, you can now have lists and planning items on your phone or personal tablet. And if you are using a cloud to connect everything, whatever you do on one, will automatically be posted on the other/s.

Besides keeping a calendar, a binder, and files, mobile electronics can be a wonderful and valuable tool that will improve your organizational skills.

And there are many new Apps to assist you. You have the Calendar, Notes and Reminder Apps that can be very valuable in your planning. You also have the camera.

The "Calendar" portion of your phone is a great place to post those important dates you must remember for the holiday season.

Often the calendar on your home or office computer will link to your phone via your computer's or phone's cloud program.

If you use Google Calendar, that too will link to most calendar Apps.

The "Notes" app in your phone is a great place to create all kinds of holiday lists shopping lists, gift lists and to save those ideas that pop into your head and you don't want to forget.

Each day I review my notes and try to act on those that need immediate attention. The goal is to clear the notes as I handle them.

Once I have made an action on a note, I can delete it. I don't delete anything until I have acted-on or transferred the note to one of my project lists.

Sometimes the notes are ideas of a gift for someone, or a menu item that I think guests will like. And sometimes it is just simply adding an item to my grocery shopping list.

When you get a fantastic idea or thought, and that little "light bulb" above your head lights up, you often want to quickly write it down before you forget it. Why not grab your phone and add the idea to one of your lists?

Some phones have an assistant or app that you can talk to, such as 'Cirri' with the iPhones or Alexa with Echo. You can call her and ask that she add an item to your notes, or shopping list, set an alarm or schedule a reminder to your calendar.

Some phones also have voice dictation that allows you to dictate notes and messages. It allows you to dictate your thoughts instead of typing them. I also use it to dictate texts and emails as it is easier that typing on the phone.

I multi-task too much. As I get older, I realize that I cannot multi-task as much as I have in my younger years. It often leads to forgetting something.

I have found many of these Apps a very valuable tool in helping me to remember and not forget.

These Apps, the Binder, the Calendar, and the Files (That's A, B, C and F) will all be very valuable in your goals to "Surviving the Holidays."

Finally, I have one more item that I hope you can use in your planning.

It is the "Get a Head Start Planning Guide," a special worksheet with 8 questions that, when answered, will help you plan and organize anything. You will find the guide later in this book

In fact, you don't have to use it just at the Holiday Season. You can use it year-round for all kinds of projects and activities.

7 UN-CLUTTER YOUR LIFE

Now, before you begin some of your planning, I would like to suggest or propose something different to the basic steps in planning.

You need to lighten up! Get rid of unwanted baggage! Throw away anything that will hold you back or bog you down.

I like to think of this as "Un-Cluttering your Life."

Steve is one of those fellows, that is so busy when the holidays arrive, that he often gets sick, or depressed, or both.

It's a result of worry. Worrying that he won't finish everything he needs to do for the holidays.

He has a great job in the city, a wonderful home, his wife and two kids. It's the average family. And of course, there is lots to do every day and every week.

But, when Thanksgiving arrives, and the holiday season begins, usually a four to six-week period, all the holiday activities, tasks and responsibilities are piled on top of the regular daily and weekly tasks.

There is his list of holiday things to do around the house; requests to visit relatives; family obligations; and of course, shopping for gifts, etc.

All of this is stacked on top of his regular job and the husband/father every-day commitments. So he worries.

Additionally, some of these new items also come with special priorities that may, in some cases, require fitting into an already tight schedule and possibly moving the regular tasks.

And the worry of doing all of this creates pressure on Steve to get everything done and to do a good job. The result is, he stresses out.

This is a common trait of those who try to please everyone and who try to accomplish more than they can handle.

In addition to everything else Steve does, after the holiday season, he is exhausted and sometimes depressed.

Much of this book is about planning and organizing parts of your life, so that your holiday season is stress-free. I gave Steve a copy of this book and I do hope it will help him.

Before the planning begins, I suggested to Steve, and now to you, to "Un-Clutter your Life."

Take a little time to look back on past years when you celebrated Christmas or Hanukkah. Think about what was good and what went wrong. I also suggest you consider what activities or tasks you might be able to reduce, delegate or delete.

This is a key element to reducing your work load and lessening the worry of trying to do everything.

You simply get rid of tasks, events and anything else that you find un-necessary.

Maybe this is not you. But I will guess that somewhere you have little items or tasks that create similar worry, possibly on a smaller scale.

It happens to almost all of us.

Maybe you can start by getting rid of anything you don't need. Old ornaments that are broken or cracked. Strings of Lights that don't work. Decorations that look stale or old.

If there is something you did not use last year, or in year's past, maybe you should throw it out or donate it to a charity.

Then move onto your schedule for the season. What activities or events can you skip or delete. What tasks or chores can you drop or eliminate?

Can you kindly pass or skip someone's party invitation? Do you need to spend days baking those special cookies or favorite dishes? Or, can you buy some cookies, etc.?

If you host holiday parties, maybe you can combine them into one fabulous party. Why plan two or three events when you can combine them and only plan one!

Sometimes the way to unclutter is to look at your daily or weekly tasks and see if there is another family member who can help you. Maybe you can delegate or pass some of the responsibility on to someone else. Reduce your work load.

Now forgive me if it sounds like I am suggesting that you drop-out of the Holiday Season all-together. That is not the purpose of this chapter.

As I said before, what I want is to help you lighten your load. Get rid of non-essential things. Find someone else to do something for you. Why not figure out how to do something earlier in the year or the season.

In eliminating what I call the minor things, you can put the focus on those things that are more important.

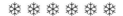

8 CREATE A PLAN

I do hope the last few chapters did not scare you off, or have you think there was too much to do. Heaven knows I do not wish to put a damper on your goal to enjoy the holidays.

Rather, I hope I have excited you with how simple it is. Yes, it does take a little more time. But, you still will be doing everything you did before. But now, in a more organized manner.

That is the secret to getting ahead and "Surviving the Holidays."

There are both similarities, and differences, between trying to get ahead during the Holiday Season and planning a wedding or major event. They both take some extra time, and there are often many details to think about, or plan for.

The same is true if you are planning events for work, or school or your church. The key element to all of them is time, how much do you have, and how are you going to use it.

So even though this book is all about the Holidays, you can still take some of the tools and suggestions and, if you so choose, apply them to other projects, events and activities.

In fact, I also think that these items are great tools to share with your children. I believe teaching them early in life, how to organize and plan, can give them a good base for the future.

This is something that, unless you are in a Scouting program, Junior Achievement, or another similar program, is normally not learned until you get into college or even after you get out of college.

ONE MORE TOOL – THE PLANNING GUIDE

Before we get to the monthly checklists, of things to do, I have one more item you may want to add to the tools I gave you in the earlier chapters

I have created a simple planning guide to assist anyone in trying to plan and organize for the holidays.

The development of this guide has come from my many years of planning projects, working on community events and doing tasks around the house.

Some ideas for this guide came from my activities in college, time in the military and Dale Carnegie training. But most came from my years as a member and officer with the Junior Chamber of Commerce, The Jaycees.

The Jaycee's gave their members a "Chairman's Planning Guide." It was a simple tool for planning any project or activity. Over the years, as I became a professional fundraiser, major event planner and television producer, I used the steps of the guide in my planning and preparations.

I thought I when I retired, I would be done with the planning guide. But surprisingly, I have easily incorporated it into many of my activities and projects. And I have shared it with friends. Now I want to share it with you.

From planning things, as simple as a banquet, or as complicated as having tens of thousands of children and adults participate in a statewide walk-a-thon, this guide was the starting point. And now I have simplified it and adapted it for you.

As I said earlier, when it comes down to the basics, it is just managing your time and simple planning.

To start you out, the "Get a Head Start Planning Guide," is just that. It is a guide that shows you what you to think about and look for as you are planning for the holidays. It is a tested guide that is based on what many folks do in preparing for a task or event.

You may find that some of the guide is a bit too much for what you want to do. If that is so, toss out what you don't need. Make it your planning guide. Re-name it if you want, "Susie's Planning Guide."

Some of the tasks you want to do, or are considering, may seem to be a bit too much.

The guide may show you that if you list the steps or list the items or materials; if you assign some of the work to someone else; or hire a service; if you break it down to smaller items and mini-tasks, it may make that project easier to accomplish.

The guide may also help you decide that the task, or an item, is out of your realm, or not necessary, and that you should forget it, save it for another year, or toss it out.

I suggest that you start with one of your smaller or simpler activities or tasks. This is your training program. Review the Planning Guide and simply review and answer the eight questions as they relate to that task.

When you do this, it often makes the task quite easy. And as you do more of the smaller tasks, you will gain confidence and experience and can move up to the larger tasks.

The nice part is that the questions are always the same. No matter what the size of the task.

Each question is listed in the next chapter, along with some sample answers.

However, since you will be working on a collection of tasks you are going to need more room to write your answers. There is not enough room on the sample guide.

So, I have done two things for you. First, I have added the guide, with room to make notes, at the back of this book. You can copy the pages and then begin filling them out.

Secondly, for those who like the internet or who are computer savvy, I have also put two versions of this guide on my web site as downloadable documents.

One is a PDF form with each of the questions followed by a lined area where you can hand-write your notes.

The second is a 'word' document that you can download into your computer or tablet. Then you can review the eight questions, fill in answers and as you progress, edit on your computer.

You can find both downloadable guides at: http://www.nationalsanta.com/project-or-task-planning-guide/

If you have multiple projects, you can make a copy for each task.

I recommend that you put these pages in your binder. If you wish, pick up some tabbed dividers to separate the tasks. Having everything, including all your planning guides, in one place, is also a stress reducer.

"Nothing is difficult when you have a plan."

9 PLANNING GUIDE SAMPLE

Now, let's look at the Planning Guide. There are eight simple question, that when answered, give you "your" plan and what to organize for an event or activity.

Often the information or answers in the planning guide are how you collect information or data for your calendar, shopping lists, budget sheet, etc.

Items needed can be added to a shopping list. Activities and tasks maybe copied over to your master calendar. When it comes to expenses, you might want to copy over the costs to a single budget sheet in your binder.

Each task and activity can be looked at using the Planning Guide.

When you look at a task and review the questions, you will get the answers you need. And then you can decide how you wish to handle something.

And the best part is when you know how you are going to handle something, there is less worry and less stress.

Below is an Example of how to use the planning guide. I have selected a simple task that many hate to do, but need to do before decorating the house, "Going through all the old Christmas Decorations."

----

1. What is the primary activity or task for this area? This is mini description of what will be going on. It gives a focus to what is to be accomplished.

- "Go through old Christmas Decorations, decide on what to keep; what to throw away or donate; and to make a list of what to buy for this year"

2. What are the specific goals to be accomplished? Here is where we start getting into details. How many people will be involved? List what elements will be completed.

- Have whole family help (Assign jobs or areas to work in)

- Go through boxes in Garage /Attic / Basement / Closets / etc.

- Organize, untangle and sort everything (i.e., take a thick piece of cardboard, 6" x 12" and wrap a string of lights around it. It will be much easier to use when you actually start decorating)

- Decide what we should get rid of, trash or to donate. (old ornaments, strings of lights, things that are missing parts, etc.)

- Decide what we are going to keep and where we are going to use the.

- Make a list of items you want to add this year (New ornaments, new lights, special decorations)

- Clean or dust items we are keeping. Often, we take everything down and just pack it away. (It is a lot easier to wash or clean in the summer and wrap in tissue paper, ready to use, than it is when it gets cold!)

- Make a list of all decorations and where you are putting them. Then when November arrives, you can quickly find them.

3.   What are the specific manpower assignments? Make a list of jobs, duties, tasks, and assignments.   (Put names with them)

- Mom - Clear the Patio as an area to sort everything. Also have labels and markers to identify boxes. Make lists of what you are keeping, what you are throwing away and what you are donating. (tax deduction)

- Dad - Possibly pick up extra clear plastic bins to sort and then store items. When finished take old stuff to Goodwill or Salvation Army.

- Tommy - Get all items out of attic, Basement and Garage. Also have trash cans or large plastic bags for throwing out old stuff.

- Susie and Mary, Look for old gift wrap in closets and under beds.

4.   What materials and supplies will be needed? Think about your Activity. Pretend that you are already there and walk through what everyone will be doing. As you do this list materials and supplies you will need. Use checklists to help yourself and your volunteers in making sure nothing was forgotten, anything we might need.

- Large Trash bags

- Tape, masking and packing

- Scissors,

- Razor knife

- Extra boxes or clear plastic storage bins

- Window Cleaner Spray, Floral Cleaning Spray, etc.

- Tablet and Paper – for notes on what we have and what we need to think about buying

5.   What other resources will be used? Write down the things, supplies, equipment you will need. Review your checklist and single out items you know you can borrow, have the hotel supply or bring from home.

- Goodwill, Salvation Army or charity to pick up items or where we can drop them off.

6.   What problems do you anticipate needing to overcome in order to successfully complete this task? This exercise is sometimes call negative brainstorming. Think of all the things that could interfere or go wrong with your activity. Then outline alternative methods to overcome each problem.

- What is the problem? Can you fix it? Will you need to cancel it? When you discuss possible problems early-on, and develop solutions or answers, you eliminate many of the worries of an activity, that can

  Worrying about possible or unknown problems can bog down all your work and put a cloud over all your activities. If you have a worry, or keep thinking about what might go wrong, you need to address it.

  The problem may never arise. It may never happen. But, knowing you have a plan somewhere, to handle the problem will allow you to concentrate and focus on other activities and ultimately have a great holiday season.

- One other part of this review may be that you decide to drop or eliminate a task, as it is unnecessary, or possibly too difficult. There is nothing wrong with making changes and eliminating something that you find unnecessary.

7. **List the specific steps to be taken.** What steps do you need to make to bring this Activity to a successful competition? Sometimes you can make a task simpler by breaking down the work into smaller tasks. Create a time line.

8. **What are the costs?** If there are costs, say for the materials and supplies you need list them here. If you need to buy something, add it here. It needs to be in your budget. Think of food for meals: boxes, paper and gift wrap; gifts to order, decorations; postage and shipping, etc., even donations you might want to make. This is an optional part of planning. But often know how much you

will be spending will help you decide on whether to do the task or eliminate it. The key thing in not stressing is not getting in over your head, either in having too much work to do or spending money you really don't have.

Now, continue through this book and begin making your plans! I do hope that this guide will be valuable for you and will help you reduce the stress of planning, organizing and making decisions.

❄ ❄ ❄ ❄

10 CHRISTMAS WISHES – YOUR CHECKLISTS

As you are planning and reading through this book, little things may pop into your head.

- Ideas for meals.

- A unique way of decorating.

- Or a special gift for someone.

- Maybe it is an event or task that needs to be considered.

And sometimes the thought that pops up, is not something you can do now, but that you 'wish' you could do.

These thoughts or ideas often come to mind as you are working on a related area or project. So, it is easy to "insert here." Most new thoughts can be added to existing places in your files or on your calendar.

But, what about those ideas or dreams of unique activities or things to do. What if the thought does not fit into your schedule, or your calendar, or even your budget. But, your mind is saying, I would love to do it.

These new ideas or visions have grabbed you and now they are something want to do. And because this book is about the holidays, I believe we should call them "Wishes."

Wishes can come at any time. They don't wait until you are sitting at your desk or in front of your computer. Often these ideas or wishes suddenly appear.

They will even pop into your head while you are sleeping. Or trying to get to sleep.

If this is you, consider having something near your bed to take notes on.

I would hope you do something to develop or create a way to collect and keep these thoughts and ideas.

One way is to create a note section in your binder. Just set up a section with pages where you can easily write down a short note. This only needs to be a few key words about your idea or thought.

And they can be about anything. Even thoughts of something that is way out of your realm, but that you would love to do someday. Maybe not this year, or even the next. But something you wish to do.

Often these 'way-out' ideas help to stimulate other ideas and surprisingly, lead to great new ideas.

You can put your notes on paper, or what I suggest, use your computer.

Create a Pinterest File

You may also want to consider starting a Pinterest file, a place to catalogue your ideas and intentions. Pinterest also allows you to search the web for ideas and to divide your ideas into sections or sub- files.

When you click on a photo or file for an idea or item, you get more information from a supporting web page or web site. And there is a button on your screen that invites you to copy the ideas to your Pinterest files.

You can have sub files for gift ideas, decorating ideas, meals and special party foods, etc. The use is unlimited.

But whatever format you use, you need to have a "wish list."

11 SOME TIME FOR YOURSELF

A unique element of the human persona, something that is very inherent in our make-up, is that we are a very generous and compassionate species.

Yes, there is something within us that allows us to instinctively look to giving, caring and helping others.

But sometimes we give so much to others while forgetting our own needs. And that is the reason for this chapter. We need to set aside some time for ourselves.

Within us all there lies the trait of giving to others, with no desire to be given something in return. It is this element of giving, of generosity that makes us a bit different from other species.

This is not to say that other selected other species do not have similar traits, but we are blessed that God gave us this wonderful piece of our personality.

Aren't we fortunate to have this? Isn't it wonderful that we can experience the wonderful feelings of giving? Sometimes even feeling that little 'tingle' inside when we have done something wonderful.

That is what makes us different and allows us to have special compassion for others.

Now when it comes to the holiday season, we tend to expand on this spirit of giving. Sometimes so much that we tend to go overboard in what we are doing. What we are giving. And how much time we are Giving

To this we add our daily schedules and the many holiday activities we squeeze in. Often, we tend to give so much time that we can be a bit exhausted at the end of the season.

That is why I believe that each of us should schedule a little time just for ourselves.

ADDING TIME JUST FOR YOU

Yes, I believe we all need to schedule a little time during the holidays just for ourselves. And sometimes I even think some personal time after the holiday season.

This time is just for us. Time to relax. Time to do something personal. Time to give back ourselves.

Please know, this is not being selfish. It is doing something to help us relax, to cope with the daily pressures, and to help us handle all the extra tasks and chores that we have added to the normal day to day activities.

I have found over the years, that I had piled so many things on my lists and schedules, that the stress was extreme.

But, when I added a few tasks or items that were personal in nature, some of the stress was reduced.

Once I realized what I was doing, I made it a plan to keep these extra tasks in my annual schedule. In fact, I actually spread them out a bit to cover the entire season. In some cases instead of just scheduling a few hours, I scheduled an entire day to do something just for myself.

I invite you to do the same.

Your personal time can be just a few minutes of quiet somewhere. Or, it could be making appointments for those little things that make life more enjoyable.

- Schedule your visits to the beauty salon. I suggest making all your appointments in advance. The salons get booked up very quickly during the holidays, especially for the weekends.

- The same goes for your manicures and pedicures. Get your appointments early.

- Visit a Day Spa or get a massage. (I actually visit my Chiropractor for an adjustment, which usually includes heat packs and a massage.)

- Spend a morning or afternoon donating your time to a local charity. Help sort donations at a food bank. Serve meals at a homeless shelter. Doing activities like this not only helps reduce stress, but it makes you feel good, too!

- And if the above idea of donating some time sounds good, maybe you want to take that extra step and possible donate some blood. This is one of the greatest gifts you can give. (December is often a month of blood shortages. So, donating now is an added gift.)

PREVENTING THE POST SEASON CRASH

Aside from what you do during the holiday season, I would like to suggest that you consider doing something for yourself after the holidays.

Schedule a few days to travel or do something special and to keep yourself busy.

Some of us tend to over work and push ourselves to our limits during the holidays. Often, our drive and spirit help us go beyond our normal work, to the extent that we are overworked and stretched to our limits.

Yet, our internal drive, our and metabolism and our immune system, seem adjust and go into overdrive to help us to make it through to the end, and that final day of celebration.

Whether it is the worry of finishing what we set our to do, or a special force or focus within us, we push right through to the end of the season. And surprisingly, during these hectic days, our immune system seems to ward off the colds and other seasonal illnesses.

And the following day, after it everything is over, we relax. Often, we totally shut down.

And when this happens, our immune system shuts down, too. And the colds and flu and other seasonal maladies seem to invade our bodies.

That is why I truly believe that we need to have something to do immediately after the holidays. Nothing big or as involved as our holiday activities. But something we can focus on and that will keep us busy for a few days, while we unwind from the whirlwind of the Holidays.

HOW TO UNWIND AFTER THE HOLIDAYS

Ever noticed that after a busy day at some activity or maybe attending a major sporting event, that you are all stressed or keyed up? And before you can go to sleep you need to unwind?

Well the same type of thing can happen when you are busy planning and working during the holidays. You push yourself, over exert yourself, get excited and have lots of ups and downs.

And afterwards you need to unwind.

It is the same feeling you might have after returning from a nice vacation. You almost need a second vacation to re-cover from the first!

I have had the same problem. After 40+ days of busy holiday work, parties, parades and events, I have had lots of adrenalin highs and morning after downs.

It is very similar to a rock star in a concert. You have the exciting highs from your performance and then you must unwind. and the following morning can be a bit depressing. These ups and down can wear on you.

And then I reach Christmas Day, the finish line, the end of my holiday season. And I am ready to relax.

For many years, the day after Christmas I crashed, physically and mentally. Sometimes I wanted to sleep for a few days. I totally disappeared from my family.

And during this time, as I shut down, my immune system relaxed and shut down, too!

This immediately allowed a cold or even worse, the flu to get into my system.

After a few years of this, I decided to do something about it. I learned that you need to have something to focus on following your big event.

Nothing big, mind you, just some activity or function that will keep you active and keep your immune system running at a normal pace.

So, I worked with my wife and we planned a small family vacation. Because of my busy schedule visiting other families, I had neglected my own family and had missed being with them.

So, scheduling an after Christmas activity or mini vacation seemed the perfect thing for all of us. Now, in addition to my December focus on the Holiday parties and events, I now had a follow up focus on the family vacation.

In doing this, I could, immediately after Christmas, put my focus and energy on the family vacation. And by not totally slowing down or shutting down, I could still relax and was not as tired as in past years. I also found my immune system stayed active and there was no after Christmas cold or illness

So, my suggestion to you is to plan for some after Holiday activities.

❄ ❄ ❄ ❄ ❄

12 STARTING IN SEPTEMBER

Many folks often wait until after Labor Day has passed before they even begin thinking about the Holiday season. They like to wait until after the summer has passed, vacations are over, and the kids are going back to school.

Others may want to wait until October and they are settled in following the summer activities. The next chapter is for those wanting to start in October.

And still there are others who like to start earlier, so later in this book I have chapters for starting in July or August. But for now, let's look at starting in September.

This is the time when we start packing away and storing the summer items and a good time to begin pulling out the items you need for fall and winter.

My Checklist for September is very similar to the other checklists in this book. However, it has been tailored just for starting in September.

Starting now, you have four months to accomplish everything. So, let's get started!

The first thing you need to do is make a list of every task or activity you feel you need to do, or want to accomplish, during the holiday season.

Secondly, using your calendar and a pencil, block out all the mandatory daily and weekly activities,

Next, add any holiday tasks, family events. And if you are a Santa, like me, any special bookings or parties that you will be attending.

This will take a little work and may require some adjustments or changes.

Now, start reviewing the schedule below. It's a simple tool you can adjust to fit your needs. You can add or subtract to start tailoring your personalized schedule.

You may want to move some things around. If you think of something else, slip it into the schedule. If something doesn't apply to your situation, delete it. When possible, I suggest you get other family members involved in the tasks and planning.

September

- Go through the attic, the basement, your closets and under the stairwells, and make a list of all you holiday decorations, lights, etc. If you can, try to put all of it in one location, so you don't have to run all over the house.

  Also, when everything is together, you are less prone to forget something.

- Decide what you want to keep and what you want to get rid of those that have grown out of style. But don't go overboard, Remember, most pre-1950 decorations and toys are now valuable collectables. Have a garage or yard sale to get rid of what you don't want. (It's 'Merge and Purge' time!)

- Make a list of those decorations that you would like to add this year. Then in late September and October, when you are out and about, you will know what you need to purchase. Many shops have pre-season sales on decorations, candles, lights, etc. And the most popular decorations disappear quickly.

- If you include an annual letter with your Christmas cards, start writing it now while things that have happened this year are still fresh in your mind. Simply add to or edit the letter each month until it's time to mail them.

- Update your holiday card mailing list. Decide what kind of and how many cards you'll want this year. Creating this list now, makes it easier to update each month, instead of trying to pull everything together later.

- Decide what kind of and how many cards you'll want this year.

- Setup a Christmas gift idea file. Use a separate page or folder for each person on your list and start clipping catalog pages, pictures from magazines, and Sunday newspaper inserts.

- Make out a list of the things you would like to do this Holiday Season, i.e.: attend a holiday concert; see a live performance of the 'Nutcracker,' visit a theme park or Holiday Village.

- If you are planning to travel, you should be searching now for travel bargains on airfare, hotels, etc. The longer you wait, the higher the prices will be as the holidays approach. If you are driving to an unknown location or place that is new to you, check the internet or the auto club for maps and directions.

- Order your holiday cards if you have them professionally printed. Get your holiday picture taken if you include a family photo with your cards. Note: Many local photo studios have special packages for holiday family Portraits. (Some even have photos with Santa!)

- Start shopping for new holiday decorations. Some shops, and especially catalogues, have pre-season sales on decorations, candles, lights, etc.

- September is also a great month for everyone to start working on their Holiday Diets. (Santa's are exempt from this!)

October

- Update your calendar. Include all personal and family activities, school & religious events, business trips, family trips, concerts, socials, annual parties, etc.

- Decide where you will be spending the holidays and make the necessary arrangements. If it's at home, set up your menu and decoration plans. If it's away, double-check school, work and social schedules that may conflict with your travel plans. Now is also a good time to slip in a few scheduled breaks, especially if your calendar is getting full.

- Scheduled a day or days, in December, to bake cookies, make fudge, wrap presents, deliver gifts, etc.

- Start ordering gifts, especially ones that require special touches or that may be going overseas. Complete any catalog or online holiday ordering now before the November rush.

- Purchase Christmas stamps for the cards, labels for the computer, and holiday pocket cards for cash gifts

- You might want to start buying a few gift cards ($$$) each month. Chose popular department and specialty stores, your friends and family shop at. Gift cards are now a very popular form of giving, as they eliminate awkward situation of giving the wrong gift. Check and make sure the gift cards have no expiration dates. Note: Those receiving gift cards will get a bonus when taking advantage of after Christmas Sales!

- Hallmark often creates a special Holiday Planning Calendar that they give away to customers. Check to see if you can get one.

- Purchase Christmas stamps for the cards, labels for the computer, holiday pocket cards for cash gifts. The U.S. Postal Service always has new holiday stamps. Annually they issue two holiday stamp sets in October. For 2018 they have a special set of four stamps featuring famous Coca-Cola Santas created by Haddon Sundblom.

  And, sometime in November or early December, the Postal Service will also have Christian, Hanukkah, Kwanza and other seasonal postage stamps.

  If you need holiday-type stamps before October, the Postal Service sometimes has "Love" stamps or other lightly themed stamps that might work. In past year's stamps had Teddy Bears and Toy Trucks.

- Either make your holiday labels now or start addressing envelopes. If you do a dozen or two a week, you'll be done before you know it.

- Complete any catalog or online holiday ordering now before the November rush.

- Start looking or rolls of gift wrap, gift boxes and bags, etc. Also ribbon, tags, tape, etc.

- Decide now, what gifts you would like to receive. Tired of getting something you really didn't want or need? Afraid you won't have an answer when someone asks you what you want? Why not be bold this year. Make a list you can have close at hand. It can be a quick reminder to yourself, or you can give it to those you exchanged gifts with. Have a variety of gifts in different price ranges to fit everyone's wallet. Then when someone asks that dreaded question, you can either suggest a gift, or present them with your wish list.

- Review your schedule. Add a few appointments in December with yourself. These are buffer times when you can relax, get a massage, go to the movies, and reduce the stress. Plan for some quality family time, too!

- Re-check school, church or other calendars for events that may conflict with your plans.

- Get a Flu Shot. If you're a senior or someone who is very active, a flu shot can help you keep your immune system in shape. For Santa, this is especially true as he will see thousands of children during the season, thus increasing his chance of catching a cold or virus.

- Double-check the calendar for changes in school, social or business events that may conflict with your travel plans.

- Pre-schedule December days for yourself, and days to be with the family. Don't assume you can just squeeze them in.

- Make December appointments for beauty salon, barber, spa, golf, etc., before their appointment calendars fill up.

November

- Address the rest of your holiday cards before Thanksgiving.

- Proofread your holiday letter one last time, print and insert into cards or envelopes ready to mail.

- Order any special gift certificates or purchase additional gift cards you may want to give. (Note: It is always good to have a few extra gift cards or gifts on hand for those surprise guest that show up, or for anyone you may have forgotten.

- Start pre-wrapping those gifts you already have. Starting early on this is one of the most important ways of reducing holiday stress. Make sure you have them well identified. I suggest a little I.D in ink somewhere on the bottom of the gift. In this way, you won't forget what is inside and who you were planning on giving it to.

- Send all your overseas gifts before Thanksgiving.

- Start sending all your U.S. gifts immediately after Thanksgiving.

- Review your calendar for parties and events & any changes. You may also want to look for conflicts. And remember that the day after a party or event, you may be a bit tired. So, try not to book too many events that are back to back

- Shop for any food staples or kitchen supplies you need before November 15 (Christmas is a tasty time, filled with all kinds of great food. Instead of trying to make it all, get out your recipes now and decide on your favorites. Do an inventory of the ingredients in your cupboards and stock up on what you need, when you catch a good sale.)

- Time to get your holiday decorations ready. Decide what you are going to use and where you will be putting these and the new items you bought in September.·

- Double check all your appointments for haircuts, beauty salon, etc., now through mid-December. Don't forget your pets grooming too! If you want to do something special, schedule a house cleaning company or maid service to clean you home before Thanksgiving and maybe one day in December.

- Clean the House. Make this a family project with everyone pitching in.

- Decorate the house. You decide whether to do this before Thanksgiving or after.

December

- Final check of your calendar for parties and events & changes.

- Mail your letters and cards on December 1st.

- Enjoy a day of baking or cooking your favorite treats and dishes. Make gift plates or boxes to deliver as gifts, with greetings for friends, relatives and shut-ins.

- Double check your gift lists and finish wrapping all presents before Dec 15th.

- Then, schedule a pre-Christmas massage, a day at the spa or a round of golf, or something special to de-stress, and finally . . .. pat yourself on the back for getting ahead this year!

I hope these ideas will help you to reach your holiday goals and give you more time to enjoy your family, friends and the true meanings of the Holidays.

13 STARTING IN OCTOBER

I do hope that you have not procrastinated, and that starting in October, was your original plan all along. I truly believe that everyone should start earlier in the year. If you had started in July, you would have had six months to do everything. With a few tasks each month.

But if you are planning to start in October, know that all the tasks from July, through December, will now be squeezed into just three months, with the largest portions in October and November.

One of the secrets of starting in October, is for you to be prepared to drop or delete some tasks or events. Sometimes you cannot do everything you want to do. So, you need to be more flexible and willing to pass on something or delete it from your wish list.

My advice to you is to go over your entire schedule. Make a list of every task or activity you feel you need to do, or want to accomplish, during the holiday season.

Be reasonable. Most folks, unless they have lots of help, can do everything from a six-month calendar squeezed into just three months. It will be too stressful, and you will often find that some tasks will not be successful if done in a hasty manner.

Secondly, using a calendar and a pencil, block out all the mandatory daily and weekly activities, and add the holiday tasks, family events and Santa bookings that are on your list.

This will take a little work and may require some adjustments or changes. From the schedule below, you can add or subtract to start building your own schedule. The schedule is a simple tool you can adjust to your needs.

You may want to move some things around. If you think of something else, slip it into the schedule. If something doesn't apply to your situation, delete it. When possible, I suggest you get other family members involved in the tasks and planning.

October

- Go through the attic, the basement, your closets and under the stairwells, and make a list of all you holiday decorations, lights, etc. If you can, try to put all of it in one location, so you don't have to run all over the house.

  Also, when everything is together, you are less prone to forget something.

- Decide what you want to keep and what you want to get rid of those that have grown out of style. But don't go overboard, Remember, most pre-1950 decorations and toys are now valuable collectables. Have a garage or yard sale to get rid of what you don't want. (It's 'Merge and Purge' time!)

- Make a list of those decorations that you would like to add this year. Then in late October and October, when you are out and about, you will know what you need to purchase. Many shops have pre-season sales on decorations, candles, lights, etc. And the most popular decorations disappear quickly.

- If you include an annual letter with your Christmas cards, start writing it now while things that have happened this year are still fresh in your mind. Simply add to or edit the letter each month until it's time to mail them.

- Update your holiday card mailing list. Decide what kind of and how many cards you'll want this year. Creating this list now, makes it easier to update each month, instead of trying to pull everything together later.

- Decide what kind of and how many cards you'll want this year.

- Setup a Christmas gift idea file. Use a separate page or folder for each person on your list and start clipping catalog pages, pictures from magazines, and Sunday newspaper inserts.

- Make out a list of the things you would like to do this Holiday Season, i.e.: attend a holiday concert; see a live performance of the 'Nutcracker,' visit a theme park or Holiday Village.

- If you are planning to travel, you should be searching now for travel bargains on airfare, hotels, etc. The longer you wait, the higher the prices will be as the holidays approach. If you are driving to an unknown location or place that is new to you, check the internet or the auto club for maps and directions.

- Order your holiday cards if you have them professionally printed. Get your holiday picture taken if you include a family photo with your cards. Note: Many local photo studios have special packages for holiday family Portraits. (Some even have photos with Santa!)

- Start shopping for new holiday decorations. Some shops, and especially catalogues, have pre-season sales on decorations, candles, lights, etc.

- October is also a great month for everyone to start working on their Holiday Diets. (Santa's are exempt from this!)

- Update your calendar. Include all personal and family activities, school & religious events, business trips, family trips, concerts, socials, annual parties, etc.

- Decide where you will be spending the holidays and make the necessary arrangements. If it's at home, set up your menu and decoration plans. If it's away, double-check school, work and social schedules that may conflict with your travel plans. Now is also a good time to slip in a few scheduled breaks, especially if your calendar is getting full.

- Scheduled a day or days, in December, to bake cookies, make fudge, wrap presents, deliver gifts, etc.

- Start ordering gifts, especially ones that require special touches or that may be going overseas. Complete any catalog or online holiday ordering now before the November rush.

- You might want to start buying a few gift cards ($$$) each month. Chose popular department and specialty stores, your friends and family shop at. Gift cards are now a very popular form of giving, as they eliminate awkward situation of giving the wrong gift. Check and make sure the gift cards have no expiration dates. Note: Those receiving gift cards will get a bonus when taking advantage of after Christmas Sales!

- Hallmark often creates a special Holiday Planning Calendar that they give away to customers. Check to see if you can get one.

- Purchase Christmas stamps for the cards, labels for the computer, holiday pocket cards for cash gifts. (The U.S. Postal Service always has new holiday stamps. For 2018 they have a special set of four stamps featuring famous Coca-Cola Santas created by Haddon Sundblom. They will also have Christian, Hanukkah, Kwanza and other seasonal postage stamps available)

  If you need holiday-type stamps before October, the Postal Service sometimes has "Love" stamps or other lightly themed stamps that might work. In past year's stamps had Teddy Bears and Toy Trucks.

- Either make your holiday labels now or start addressing envelopes. If you do a dozen or two a week, you'll be done before you know it.

- Start looking for rolls of gift wrap, gift boxes and bags, etc. Also ribbon, tags, tape, etc.

- Decide now, what gifts you would like to receive. Tired of getting something you really didn't want or need? Afraid you won't have an answer when someone asks you what you want? Why not be bold this year. Make a list you can have close at hand. It can be a quick reminder to yourself, or you can give it to those you exchanged gifts with. Have a variety of gifts in different price ranges to fit everyone's wallet. Then when someone asks that dreaded question, you can either suggest a gift, or present them with your wish list.

- Review your schedule. Add a few appointments in December with yourself. These are buffer times when you can relax, get a massage, go to the movies, and reduce the stress. Plan for some quality family time, too!

- Re-check school, church or other calendars for events that may conflict with your plans.

- Get a Flu Shot. If you're a senior or someone who is very active, a flu shot can help you keep your immune system in shape. For Santa, this is especially true as he will see thousands of children during the season, thus increasing his chance of catching a cold or virus.

- Pre-schedule December days for yourself, and days to be with the family. Don't assume you can just squeeze them in.

- Make December appointments for beauty salon, barber, spa, golf, etc., before their appointment calendars fill up.

November

- Address the rest of your holiday cards before Thanksgiving.

- Complete any catalog or online holiday ordering now before the Thanksgiving rush

- Proofread your holiday letter one last time, print and insert into cards or envelopes ready to mail.

- Double-check the calendar for changes in school, social or business events that may conflict with your travel plans

- Order any special gift certificates or purchase additional gift cards you may want to give. (Note: It is always good to have a few extra gift cards or gifts on hand for those surprise guest that show up, or for anyone you may have forgotten.

- Start pre-wrapping those gifts you already have. Starting early on this is one of the most important ways of reducing holiday stress. Make sure you have them well identified. I suggest a little I.D in ink somewhere on the bottom of the gift. In this way, you won't forget what is inside and who you were planning on giving it to.

- Send all your overseas gifts before Thanksgiving.

- Start sending all your U.S. gifts immediately after Thanksgiving.

- Review your calendar for parties and events & any changes. You may also want to look for conflicts. And remember that the day after a party or event, you may be a bit tired. So, try not to book too many events that are back to back

- Shop for any food staples or kitchen supplies you need before November 15 (Christmas is a tasty time, filled with all kinds of great food. Instead of trying to make it all, get out your recipes now and decide on your favorites. Do an inventory of the ingredients in your cupboards and stock up on what you need, when you catch a good sale.)

- Time to get your holiday decorations ready. Decide what you are going to use and where you will be putting these and the new items you bought in October.

- Double check all your appointments for haircuts, beauty salon, etc., now through mid-December. Don't forget your pets grooming too! If you want to do something special, schedule a house cleaning company or maid service to clean you home before Thanksgiving and maybe one day in December.

- Clean the House. Make this a family day with everyone pitching in.

- Decorate the house. You decide whether to do this before Thanksgiving or after.

December

- Final check of your calendar for parties and events & changes.

- Mail your letters and cards on December 1st.

- Enjoy a day of baking or cooking your favorite treats and dishes. Make gift plates or boxes to deliver as gifts, with greetings for friends, relatives and shut-ins.

- Double check your gift lists and finish wrapping all presents before Dec 15th.

- Then, schedule a pre-Christmas massage, a day at the spa or a round of golf, or something special to de-stress, and finally . . .. pat yourself on the back for getting ahead this year!

I hope these ideas will help you to reach your holiday goals and give you more time to enjoy your family, friends and the true meanings of the Holidays.

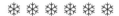

14 NOVEMBER – THE COUNTDOWN

By now, many of the tasks you started in previous months are nearing completion.

But, remember November is a 'crunch' month. Or, for some, it is the last quarter of the big game. (Did you notice I used some football metaphors in November? I just had too!)

If all goes as planned, by Thanksgiving you will have accomplished most of your holiday work. This means, other than some holiday cooking or preparing fresh meals, you are free to do what you want.

This means you will have more free time, or at least a more relaxed schedule from Thanksgiving to New Year's. Yes, you should be able to relax a little, enjoy your family, visit friends and celebrate the joys of the season.

Most of the rest of this chapter is a reminder of what you read in the previous chapters.

I mentioned some of the following items on those pages, but let me give you a few reminders of the most important November tasks:

- November is the most popular month to do your holiday decorating. So, it is time to get all the decorations we have talked about in previous chapters and create the magic around your home. Hopefully you have decided what and where you want to put out or hang, both the older items and collectibles and those new items we suggested you buy in September.

- Order any special gift certificates or purchase additional gift cards you may want to give. (Note: It is always good to have a few extra gift cards or gifts on hand for those surprise guest that show up, or for anyone you may have forgotten.)

- November is the time to do your final orders of gift baskets, flowers or candies, that are delivered direct from the source. A nice thing about this is you can pre-select the delivery dates in advance.

- Start pre-wrapping those gifts you already have. Starting early on this is one of the most important ways of reducing holiday stress. Make sure you have them well identified. I suggest a little I.D in ink somewhere on the bottom of the gift. In this way, you won't forget what is inside and who you were planning on giving it to.

- This is a time to do the final check of your pantry and cupboards. Shop for any food staples or kitchen supplies you need before November 15 (Christmas is a tasty time, filled with all kinds of great food. Instead of trying to make it all, get out your recipes now and decide on your favorites. Do an inventory of the ingredients in your cupboards and stock up on what you need, when you catch a good sale.)

- If you make fruit cakes for gifts, November is the perfect month to bake them. And if you want to know where to send Santa's fruit cake, may I suggest that you send it to a service man, a Veteran, or that neighbor down the street who can't get out.

- Mail your holiday cards and/or holiday letters before Thanksgiving. (remember you should have done all the addressing, and pre-stamped everything.)

Here is an idea you won't find in the previous chapters. Would you like to have some fun with the letters you are sending? Why not have them postmarked from the "North Pole!"

It is quite easy. Finish your cards and letters, put them in the addressed envelopes and add the necessary 'first class' postage. And don't forget your Post Office has a nice collection of holiday stamps.

Now, you do not drop these cards and letters in the mail box.

Instead, place all the pre-postaged cards and letters into a USPS Priority Mail box (Usually around $11) and mail it to "Postmaster, North Pole, AK 99705." When the postmaster receives it, they will usually hand-stamp or imprint the "North Pole" postmark on your mail!

Your friends and family (especially the kids) will be totally surprised and truly enjoy receiving your mail, from the, "North Pole!"

By the way, you can also do the same by mailing your packaged cards and letters to Postmasters, in Bethlehem, PA, Santa Claus, IN, etc.

And would you believe that someone put together a list of all the towns, hamlets and cities that have Christmas or holiday themed names. Visit: https://www.accuracyproject.org/towns-xmas.html.

- Review your calendar for parties and events & any changes. You may also want to look for conflicts. And remember that the day after a party or event, you may be a bit tired. So, try not to book too many events that are back to back

- Double check all your appointments for haircuts, beauty salon, etc., now through mid-December. Don't forget your pets grooming too! And remember, many salons, spas, groomers, etc., get booked-up quite early in the season.

- Go through your closet and plan on what you will wear to the events and parties from Thanksgiving through Christmas. (Note: If you see some clothes, shoes, etc., you know you won't be using, consider donating them to your favorite charity.)

- Clean the House. Make this a family project with everyone pitching in.

  If you want to do something special, schedule a house cleaning company or maid service to clean your home before Thanksgiving and maybe one day in December.

- Enjoy your Thanksgiving!

15 THE FINISH LINE - DECEMBER

This will be a short chapter. By now you should have done just about everything for the holidays, except your holiday baking, cooking special meals and finally, enjoying the many activities you have put on your calendar.

So, first things first. Take a deep breath, relax. You have done a great job! By the way, when you are relaxed, these final tasks really won't be a burden.

- Mail your letters and cards on December 1st.

- Make the final check of your calendar for parties and events & changes. Hopefully you also have a few days that are open, with nothing scheduled. These are your days.

  These are the days and times for you to get that pre-Christmas massage; relax while getting a mani-pedi; spend a day at the spa or a round of golf, or something special to de-stress.

  May I also suggest that you take some time to meditate and reflect. It is a wonderful way of calming one's self.

- Be sure to send all your U.S. gifts in the first week or ten days of December. Don't wait. And do not be worried that a gift arrives too early. If you don't want them to open it until Christmas Day, put a note on the package or gift. You know the note I am talking about, "DO NOT OPEN UNTIL CHRISTMAS"

- Why not use some of that free time you have to make some telephone calls to the distant family and friends that you will not see during the holidays.

  I suggest you try to do one call per day.

  This is also a wonderful gift to those who cannot travel or get out to visit. (It is also a wonderful gift for you, as you will receive a great deal of joy and love in what you are giving.)

- Enjoy a day of baking or cooking your favorite treats and dishes. Make gift plates or boxes to deliver as gifts, with greetings for friends, relatives and shut-ins.

- And, pat yourself on the back for getting ahead this year!

16 FOR THOSE WHO CAN'T WAIT "STARTING IN JULY"

Now, if you are one of those true early birds, then this added chapter is for you.

July is often looked at as the major 'Vacation" month. Thus, starting your holiday planning in July, allows you to take a little more time and work a bit slower, at a very relaxed pace. You have six months, half of the year, to plan you holiday activities.

With a little advanced planning, spread out between July and Christmas, you too can reduce stress and have more time to enjoy the holiday season.

The first thing you need to do is make a list of every task or activity you feel you need to do, or want to accomplish, during the holiday season.

Secondly, using a calendar and a pencil, block out all the mandatory daily and weekly activities, and add the holiday tasks, family events and Santa bookings that are on your list.

This will take a little work and may require some adjustments or changes. From the schedule below, you can add or subtract to start building your own schedule. The schedule is a simple tool you can adjust to your needs.

You may want to move some things around. If you think of something else, slip it into the schedule. If something doesn't apply to your situation, delete it. When possible, I suggest you get other family members involved in the tasks and planning.

July

- Go through the attic, the basement, your closets and under the stairwells, and make a list of all you holiday decorations, lights, etc. If you can, try to put all of it in one location, so you don't have to run all over the house.

  Also, when everything is together, you are less prone to forget something.

- Make a close look at your holiday decorations and lights. Decide what you want to keep and what you want to get rid of those that have grown out of style. But don't go overboard, Remember, most pre-1950 decorations and toys are now valuable collectables. Have a garage or yard sale to get rid of what you don't want. (It's 'Merge and Purge' time!)

- Start making your list of those decorations that you would like to add this year. Then in late September and October, when you are out and about, you will know what you need to purchase. Many shops have pre-season sales on decorations, candles, lights, etc. And the most popular decorations disappear quickly.

- If you include an annual letter with your Christmas cards, start writing it now while things that have happened this year are still fresh in your mind. Simply add to or edit the letter each month until it's time to mail them.

August

- Update your holiday card mailing list. Decide what kind of and how many cards you'll want this year. Creating this list now, makes it easier to update each month, instead of trying to pull everything together later.

- Decide what kind of and how many cards you'll want this year.

- Setup a Christmas gift idea file. Use a separate page or folder for each person on your list and start clipping catalog pages, pictures from magazines, and Sunday newspaper inserts.

- Make out a list of the things you would like to do this Holiday Season, i.e.: attend a holiday concert; see a live performance of the 'Nutcracker,' visit a theme park or Holiday Village.

September

- Update your calendar. Include all personal and family activities, school & religious events, business trips, family trips, concerts, socials, annual parties, etc.

- Hallmark often creates a special Holiday Planning Calendar that they give away to customers. Check to see if you can get one.

- Scheduled a day or days, in December, to bake cookies, make fudge, wrap presents, deliver gifts, etc.

- Decide where you will be spending the holidays and make the necessary arrangements. If it's at home, set up your menu and decoration plans. If it's away, double-check school, work and social schedules that may conflict with your travel plans. Now is also a good time to slip in a few scheduled breaks, especially if your calendar is getting full.

- If you are planning to travel, you should be searching now for travel bargains on airfare, hotels, etc. The longer you wait, the higher the prices will be as the holidays approach. If you are driving to an unknown location or place that is new to you, check the internet or the auto club for maps and directions.

- Start ordering gifts, especially ones that require special touches or that may be going overseas.

- You might want to start buying a few gift cards ($$$) each month. Chose popular department and specialty stores, your friends and family shop at. Gift cards are now a very popular form of giving, as they eliminate awkward situation of giving the wrong gift. Check and make sure the gift cards have no expiration dates. Note: Those receiving gift cards will get a bonus when taking advantage of after Christmas Sales!

- Order your holiday cards if you have them professionally printed. Get your holiday picture taken if you include a family photo with your cards. Note: Many local photo studios have special packages for holiday family Portraits. (Some even have photos with Santa!)

- Start shopping for new holiday decorations. Some shops, and especially catalogues, have pre-season sales on decorations, candles, lights, etc.

- September is also a great month for everyone to start working on their Holiday Diets. (Santa's are exempt from this!)

October

- Finish ordering your gifts. Complete any catalog or online holiday ordering now before the November rush.

- Purchase Christmas stamps for the cards, labels for the computer, holiday pocket cards for cash gifts. (The U.S. Postal Service always has new holiday stamps. For 2018 they have a special set of four stamps featuring famous Coca-Cola Santas created by Haddon Sundblom. They will also have Christian, Hanukkah, Kwanza and other seasonal postage stamps available.)

  If you need holiday-type stamps before October, the Postal Service sometimes has "Love" stamps or other lightly themed stamps that might work. In past year's stamps had Teddy Bears and Toy Trucks.

- Either make your holiday labels now or start addressing envelopes. If you do a dozen or two a week, you'll be done before you know it.

- Complete any catalog or online holiday ordering now before the November rush.

- Start looking or rolls of gift wrap, gift boxes and bags, etc. Also ribbon, tags, tape, etc.

- Decide now, what gifts you would like to receive. Tired of getting something you really didn't want or need? Afraid you won't have an answer when someone asks you what you want? Why not be bold this year. Make a list you can have close at hand. It can be a quick reminder to yourself, or you can give it to those you exchanged gifts with. Have a variety of gifts in different price ranges to fit everyone's wallet. Then when someone asks that dreaded question, you can either suggest a gift, or present them with your wish list.

- Review your schedule. Add a few appointments in December with yourself. These are buffer times when you can relax, get a massage, go to the movies, and reduce the stress. Plan for some quality family time, too!

- Re-check school, church or other calendars for events that may conflict with your plans.

- Get a Flu Shot. If you're a senior or someone who is very active, a flu shot can help you keep your immune system in shape. For Santa, this is especially true as he will see thousands of children during the season, thus increasing his chance of catching a cold or virus.

- Double-check the calendar for changes in school, social or business events that may conflict with your travel plans.

- Pre-schedule December days for yourself, and days to be with the family. Don't assume you can just squeeze them in.

- Make December appointments for beauty salon, barber, spa, golf, etc., before their appointment calendars fill up.

November

- Address the rest of your holiday cards before Thanksgiving.

- Proofread your holiday letter one last time, print and insert into cards or envelopes ready to mail.

- Order any special gift certificates or purchase additional gift cards you may want to give. (Note: It is always good to have a few extra gift cards or gifts on hand for those surprise guest that show up, or for anyone you may have forgotten.

- Start pre-wrapping those gifts you already have. Starting early on this is one of the most important ways of reducing holiday stress. Make sure you have them well identified. I suggest a little I.D in ink somewhere on the bottom of the gift. In this way, you won't forget what is inside and who you were planning on giving it to.

- Send all your overseas gifts before Thanksgiving.

- Start sending all your U.S. gifts immediately after Thanksgiving.

- Review your calendar for parties and events & any changes. You may also want to look for conflicts. And remember that the day after a party or event, you may be a bit tired. So, try not to book too many events that are back to back

- Shop for any food staples or kitchen supplies you need before November 15 (Christmas is a tasty time, filled with all kinds of great food. Instead of trying to make it all, get out your recipes now and decide on your favorites. Do an inventory of the ingredients in your cupboards and stock up on what you need, when you catch a good sale.)

- Time to get your holiday decorations ready. Decide what you are going to use and where you will be putting these and the new items you bought in September.

- Double check all your appointments for haircuts, beauty salon, etc., now through mid-December. Don't forget your pets grooming too! If you want to do something special, schedule a house cleaning company or maid service to clean you home before Thanksgiving and maybe one day in December.

- Clean the House. Make this a family day with everyone pitching in.

- Decorate the house. You decide whether to do this before Thanksgiving or after.

December

- Final check of your calendar for parties and events & changes.

- Mail your letters and cards on December 1st.

- Enjoy a day of baking or cooking your favorite treats and dishes. Make gift plates or boxes to deliver as gifts, with greetings for friends, relatives and shut-ins.

- Double check your gift lists and finish wrapping all presents before Dec 15th.

- Then, schedule a pre-Christmas massage, a day at the spa or a round of golf, or something special to de-stress, and finally . . .. pat yourself on the back for getting ahead this year!

I hope these ideas will help you to reach your holiday goals and give you more time to enjoy your family, friends and the true meanings of the Holidays.

May the Joys of the Season be with you every day.

17 STARTING IN AUGUST

Not everyone wants to start thinking about the Holidays while still experiencing the warmth of summer. But, with the extra hours of daylight, there is often opportunities to begin your planning in August.

This is the most popular of the Holiday checklists as it covers a five-month period. With a little advanced planning, starting in August, you can reduce stress and have more time to enjoy the holiday season.

And for those who can't wait, and wish to start earlier, I have created a special checklist for them. Just jump to the previous chapter, "Starting in July."

Now let's look at starting in August. The first thing you need to do is make a list of every task or activity you feel you need to do, or want to accomplish, during the holiday season.

Secondly, using a calendar and a pencil, block out all the mandatory daily and weekly activities, and add the holiday tasks, family events and Santa bookings that are on your list.

This will take a little work and may require some adjustments or changes. From the schedule below, you can add or subtract to start building your own schedule. The schedule is a simple tool you can adjust to your needs.

You may want to move some things around. No Problem. If you think of something else, slip it into the schedule. If something doesn't apply to your situation, delete it. When possible, I suggest you get other family members involved in the tasks and planning.

August

- Go through the attic, the basement, your closets and under the stairwells, and make a list of all you holiday decorations, lights, etc. If you can, try to put all of it in one location, so you don't have to run all over the house.

  Also, when everything is together, you are less prone to forget something.

- Decide what you want to keep and what you want to get rid of those that have grown out of style. But don't go overboard, Remember, most pre-1950 decorations and toys are now valuable collectables. Have a garage or yard sale to get rid of what you don't want. (It's 'Merge and Purge' time!)

- Make a list of those decorations that you would like to add this year. Then in late September and October, when you are out and about, you will know what you need to purchase. Many shops have pre-season sales on decorations, candles, lights, etc. And the most popular decorations disappear quickly.

- If you include an annual letter with your Christmas cards, start writing it now while things that have happened this year are still fresh in your mind. Simply add to or edit the letter each month until it's time to mail them.

- Update your holiday card mailing list. Decide what kind of and how many cards you'll want this year. Creating this list now, makes it easier to update each month, instead of trying to pull everything together later.

- Make out a list of the things you would like to do this Holiday Season, i.e.: attend a holiday concert; see a live performance of the 'Nutcracker,' visit a theme park or Holiday Village.

- Decide what kind of and how many cards you'll want this year.

- Setup a Christmas gift idea file. Use a separate page or folder for each person on your list and start clipping catalog pages, pictures from magazines, and Sunday newspaper inserts.

September

- Update your calendar. Include all personal and family activities, school & religious events, business trips, family trips, concerts, socials, annual parties, etc.

- Hallmark often creates a special Holiday Planning Calendar that they give away to customers. Check to see if you can get one.

- Scheduled a day or days, in December, to bake cookies, make fudge, wrap presents, deliver gifts, etc.

- Decide where you will be spending the holidays and make the necessary arrangements. If it's at home, set up your menu and decoration plans. If it's away, double-check school, work and social schedules that may conflict with your travel plans. Now is also a good time to slip in a few scheduled breaks, especially if your calendar is getting full.

- If you are planning to travel, you should be searching now for travel bargains on airfare, hotels, etc. The longer you wait, the higher the prices will be as the holidays approach. If you are driving to an unknown location or place that is new to you, check the internet or the auto club for maps and directions.

- Start ordering gifts, especially ones that require special touches or that may be going overseas.

- You might want to start buying a few gift cards ($$$) each month. Chose popular department and specialty stores, your friends and family shop at. Gift cards are now a very popular form of giving, as they eliminate awkward situation of giving the wrong gift. Check and make sure the gift cards have no expiration dates. Note: Those receiving gift cards will get a bonus when taking advantage of after Christmas Sales!

- Order your holiday cards if you have them professionally printed. Get your holiday picture taken if you include a family photo with your cards. Note: Many local photo studios have special packages for holiday family Portraits. (Some even have photos with Santa!)

- Start shopping for new holiday decorations. Some shops, and especially catalogues, have pre-season sales on decorations, candles, lights, etc.

- September is also a great month for everyone to start working on their Holiday Diets. (Santa's are exempt from this!)

October

- Finish ordering your gifts. Complete any catalog or online holiday ordering now before the November rush.

    Purchase Christmas stamps for the cards, labels for the computer, holiday pocket cards for cash gifts. (The U.S. Postal Service always has new holiday stamps. They also have Hanukkah and Kwanzaa postage stamps available.)

    The U.S. Postal Service annually issues two holiday stamp sets in October. And, sometime in November or early December, the Postal Service will also be releasing special stamps with Christian, Hanukkah and Kwanzaa themes.

    If you need holiday-type stamps before October, the Postal Service sometimes has "Love" stamps or other lightly themed stamps that might work. In past year's stamps had Teddy Bears and Toy Trucks.

- Either make your holiday labels now or start addressing envelopes. If you do a dozen or two a week, you'll be done before you know it.

- Complete any catalog or online holiday ordering now before the November rush.

- Start looking or rolls of gift wrap, gift boxes and bags, etc. Also ribbon, tags, tape, etc.

- Decide now, what gifts you would like to receive. Tired of getting something you really didn't want or need? Afraid you won't have an answer when someone asks you what you want? Why not be bold this year.

  Make a list you can have close at hand. It can be a quick reminder to yourself, or you can give it to those you exchanged gifts with. Have a variety of gifts in different price ranges to fit everyone's wallet.

  Then when someone asks that dreaded question, you can either suggest a gift, or present them with your wish list.

- Review your schedule. Add a few appointments in December with yourself. These are buffer times when you can relax, get a massage, go to the movies, and reduce the stress. Plan for some quality family time, too!

- Re-check school, church or other calendars for events that may conflict with your plans.

- Get a Flu Shot. If you're a senior or someone who is very active, a flu shot can help you keep your immune system in shape. For Santa, this is especially true as he will see thousands of children during the season, thus increasing his chance of catching a cold or virus.

- Double-check the calendar for changes in school, social or business events that may conflict with your travel plans.

- Pre-schedule December days for yourself, and days to be with the family. Don't assume you can just squeeze them in.

- Make December appointments for beauty salon, barber, spa, golf, etc., before their appointment calendars fill up.

November

- Address the rest of your holiday cards before Thanksgiving.

- Proofread your holiday letter one last time, print and insert into cards or envelopes ready to mail.

- Order any special gift certificates or purchase additional gift cards you may want to give. (Note: It is always good to have a few extra gift cards or gifts on hand for those surprise guest that show up, or for anyone you may have forgotten.

- Start pre-wrapping those gifts you already have. Starting early on this is one of the most important ways of reducing holiday stress. Make sure you have them well identified. I suggest a little I.D in ink somewhere on the bottom of the gift. In this way, you won't forget what is inside and who you were planning on giving it to.

- Send all your overseas gifts before Thanksgiving.

- Start sending all your U.S. gifts immediately after Thanksgiving.

- Review your calendar for parties and events & any changes. You may also want to look for conflicts. And remember that the day after a party or event, you may be a bit tired. So, try not to book too many events that are back to back

- Shop for any food staples or kitchen supplies you need before November 15 (Christmas is a tasty time, filled with all kinds of great food. Instead of trying to make it all, get out your recipes now and decide on your favorites.

  Do an inventory of the ingredients in your cupboards and stock up on what you need, when you catch a good sale.)

- Time to get your holiday decorations ready. Decide what you are going to use and where you will be putting these and the new items you bought in September.

- Double check all your appointments for haircuts, beauty salon, etc., now through mid-December. Don't forget your pets grooming too! If you want to do something special, schedule a house cleaning company or maid service to clean you home before Thanksgiving and maybe one day in December.

- Clean the House. Make this a family day with everyone pitching in.

- Decorate the house. You decide whether to do this before Thanksgiving or after.

December

- Final check of your calendar for parties and events & changes.

- Mail your letters and cards on December 1st.

- Enjoy a day of baking or cooking your favorite treats and dishes. Make gift plates or boxes to deliver as gifts, with greetings for friends, relatives and shut-ins.

- Double check your gift lists and finish wrapping all presents before Dec 15th.

- Then, schedule a pre-Christmas massage, a day at the spa or a round of golf, or something special to de-stress, and finally . . .. pat yourself on the back for getting ahead this year!

I hope these ideas will help you to reach your holiday goals and give you more time to enjoy your family, friends and the true meanings of the Holidays.

18 THERE IS NO SANTA?

The sub-title of this book mentions reducing stress during the holidays. And although it is not usually a stressful item, there is one worry that often touches the parent or parents. It is something I often hear from parents in my holiday work as Santa

This worry is about their children growing up too fast. More importantly it's when their children tell them, they no long believe in Santa and the Magic of Christmas.

As with just about every parent throughout time, we create little white lies as part of raising our children. Some of this we do to teach and guide our children in their development.

And then there is our teaching children the legends and history of Santa Claus, hoping that they will believe in the magic. Our goal is to give them feelings of joy.

And along the way, we too enjoy wonderful feelings of joy.

Parents and Families have been experiencing this for centuries.

When the Magic is Shattered

But then, one day the magic is shattered. Most often it starts with a child announcing, "There is no Santa!"

I hope, as you read on, you will appreciate the hints and suggestions I offer. Possibly they will help soften the blow and put more meaning and "Belief" in Santa, and Christmas.

This worry of a child finding out the truth, often materializes right around the time they enter the second grade. Sometimes sooner, and maybe a year or two later.

But every parent will experience it at some time. Especially when their child is around their peers. Most often the announcement is, "My friends told me there is no Santa!"

Yes, it is usually other children of the same age, or even a year or two older who, thinking they are so smart, ruin the dream.

This worry that suddenly appears is, "how are they going to respond to their child."

What would you do if your child came home and confronted you?

Yes, it will happen sometime. There will always be a point in a child's life when the magic is broken. When the veil or cloud of imagination is diluted or dissolved.

Every child eventually hears from his friends the challenge that Santa is not real. Sometimes they are told that the parents are Santa Claus and they are hiding gifts in closets and under the beds.

I often think that any single child can play and can be creative and enjoy playing with toys or games. All by themselves. And if you get two kids together, they become a bit more creative.

But when you add a third child, I often think that third child becomes "Eddie Haskell." You remember Eddie, from the early television sitcom, "Leave it to Beaver."

Like Eddie, some of your children's peers will challenge them and demonstrate how smart they are by telling your children what's behind the curtain.

Preparing for the inevitable.

There are a couple of things you can do to soften the blow when a child hears that Santa is not real.

Your child has listened to you and believes you when you say there IS a Santa Claus. But, they also want to believe their friends. It's a dilemma.

I think one way you can prepare for that day, is to start early if you can, when the children are younger, and teach them about Secret Giving.

Tell them the story of St. Nicholas and/or Santa Claus. Teach them about how Nicholas gave away his wealth to help others and that he did it secretly.

It made Nicholas feel good. So, he taught others about secret giving and the wonderful feeling he got from giving, and how they too could feel good, too.

Let them know that St Nicholas and his descendants have been secretly giving for over seventeen centuries.

As a follow up, to telling the children about Secret Giving, you should encourage them to do something special and do a little of their own Secret Giving.

This is both a fun and rewarding thing for children to do. And you can start this when they are around four, or even pre-school age.

Their giving can be simple, like making a card for someone, or helping you to bake cookies to give to neighbors.

By teaching your children about Secret Giving, you are preparing them for that day when they start learning the truth.

When they find out the Truth

There are two avenues or directions you can go when your child tells you that he or she has heard there is no Santa.

One, you can admit the truth and tie it into the lessons you have taught about secret giving.

Two, you could tell them about the history of St. Nicholas and Santa Claus. And along the way, you insert another little white lie and tell them the following story.

St. Nicholas Many years ago, actually over 150 years ago, Santa started worrying about getting to every child on earth. So, he came up with a plan.

That year he visited all the parents and asked them for their help. These parents were your Great-Great-Great Grandparents.

Santa explained that the world population was growing, and it was getting harder and harder for him to get to everyone and deliver all the toys.

If he could reduce the number of toys for each child to two or three, he could work faster and reach more children.

So, he asked parents everywhere to help him. He invited them to join him and become secret givers to the children. They would share in the joy of secret giving by taking care of their own children. They would give some of the Christmas gifts and toys.

And Santa would deliver the big gifts.

So, the parents followed Santa's instructions. It was exciting and so much fun. They felt so good. It must be what Santa feels when he delivers the presents.

Santa also had one other instruction. One day, when the children are old enough to understand, the parents must share the secret with them.

So, when they were old enough, the parents told them of the agreement with Santa. Just as I am now telling you.

Your grandparents did this for Mommy and Daddy and now Mommy and Daddy have the joy of giving you a few gifts each Christmas. And on Christmas Eve, Santa brings the big ones.

And now I share this with you. When you grow up, and have children of your own, you too will get to help Santa by giving some of the gifts and toys to your children.

The responsibility of presenting gifts to everyone has been going on for centuries. And it will continue for many more centuries. And parents everywhere will continue helping Santa and sharing in the joy of Secret Giving.

This little ruse, or white lie, might keep the children 'Believing' for one or two additional years. Maybe even more.

Isn't it nice to keep some of the magic and innocence alive for a little longer.

Hopefully your child will continue believing. Of course, there will be another day in the future, when your child finally uncovers the real secret.

At that time they will really know the answer, the real secret. This is the time to congratulate them on learning the surprise of secret giving.

Further, you can now explain to them that since they know the secret, they must become one of the Secret Givers and must now start their own annual program of secret giving.

Hopefully, if followed, your child will enjoy the aspects of secret giving.

And you have now guaranteed that this centuries-old tradition will continue forever.

23 THE VISIT TO SANTA

Handy Hints for Families visiting Santa

Each year millions of families make the annual trek to their local mall, for the traditional photo with the man in the red suit.

For some it is a fun experience. For others, just the opposite. And in between there are hundreds, if not thousands, of variations to what a visit might be like.

As one who has seen these variations, I have tried to find out what makes or creates a successful visit. I have talked with thousands of families and Santas, too! In doing so, I have collected some wonderful advice that I wish to share with everyone.

- Before deciding on what day to get your photos, check with the mall. Are there hours when the lines are shorter? Do they offer appointments or special scheduling? Some malls use two or more Santas. (Please, don't tell anyone!) You may want to find out when your favorite Santa is sitting in the chair.

- Make it a fun activity – It should be like going to Disneyland. When getting your children ready, try to make this a fun activity. If they are having fun, the photos will be more natural and much better.

- When dressing your children, don't force them to wear something they don't like. This will just put them in a bad mood and it will show in your photo. If they dress comfortably, the photos will be more natural and often more alive.

  NOTE: Some of the greatest baby or toddler photos are those when the shoes and socks are off. One of my favorites is with a seven-month-old who is just wearing a diaper with green velvet cover.

- Give yourself plenty of time. Trying to rush creates tension and leads to stress. Set aside an entire morning or afternoon to make your trip to Santa, and maybe do some family shopping or sightseeing.

- Prepare your children - Make sure they are ready to visit Santa. A visit with Santa Claus can be quite scary for a small child.

- In preparation of going to see Santa Claus, read some books to your child about Santa. Let them see pictures of Santa or watch a cartoon about Santa and his Reindeer.

- Before taking your child to the line, let them observe how other kids are standing in line waiting to sit on Santa Claus' lap.

- When it is time for pictures with Santa Claus, if your child is too scared, consider doing a group photo with you holding your child or have your child stand next to Santa Claus.

- Talk to your children about the spirit of giving. You know they are also visiting Santa to tell him what they want for Christmas.

  Children may spend hours, days, even weeks thinking about what they want for Christmas, and what they will tell Santa when they see him.

  While driving to see Santa, or waiting in line, talk to you children about what Santa means. Simply stated, Santa represents, love, joy and giving.

  Whether you are Christian or not, you can explain to your children that Christmas is not, just a time for getting, it's also a time for giving. Sometimes, it's a time for secret giving.

  Ask them if they know someone they should give something to. Would they like to give something secretly?

- Before you leave the house, Santa recommends that you bring along a comb or brush; hairspray; moist towelettes; and pins or barrettes for long hair. Kids can surprise all of us.

- The best photos are taken in the first five to ten seconds. This is especially true with babies and nervous children. Help seat your children and then quickly back out of the photo area. After the photo, Santa can talk to the children.

If you have a newborn to six-month-old baby, you should take the baby up to Santa. Seat any other children in your family first and then give the baby to Santa last. Then let the photographer take the photos. After the photo is taken, you can remove the baby and Santa can talk with the other children.

- If your child is afraid of Santa, never force them to sit on Santa's lap. This can be a very traumatic experience. Of course, I have had hundreds of parents still request the photos even if they child is crying or screaming. I think they are planning on saving the photo until their child is older and they can embarrass them!

- If your child has a wet bottom, let Santa and his helpers know. If Santa's suit gets wet or soiled, everything must stop while he changes or cleans up. Ask Santa's helper if you can pass on your photo until your child is changed. They should give you the OK to come back to the front of the line.

By considering the suggestions above, you may find that your annual visit to Santa is more fun for your children, more meaningful and a joy for you.

©Copyright 2003, 2017 Timothy Connaghan

❄ ❄ ❄ ❄ ❄ ❄

20 WHEN SANTA VISITS YOU

Handy Hints for a Visit from Santa

In the previous chapter I covered some details and gave some suggestions in planning a visit to Santa, at a Mall or community event. But maybe you would like to do something more personal for your family and friends.

What about hiring Santa to come directly to your home or business? This chapter will cover the details of arranging for a Santa to visit you. A checklist for a personal visit is included at the end of this chapter.

For hundreds of years, long before we would see Santa at a department store or mall, families enjoyed and celebrated the arrival of St. Nicholas to their town or village.

Over the centuries, he, or one of his descendants, began making personal visits to home and neighborhood gatherings.

Often the holiday visitor was someone's uncle or possibly grandfather. It was a very special event, and it created a strong reinforcement to the Christmas Season and Secret Giving.

Today that tradition continues as Santa Claus not only appears at malls, but now he makes personal visits to homes and businesses. Sometimes he even brings Mrs. Claus.

Now you might think that this type of visit is only for those who can afford it. But, it is not. By having a couple of families join together to hire Santa, for a family or neighborhood party, they pool their monies and the cost is often less per family, than what you might pay for that two or three-minute visit at the mall.

So, instead of one or two minutes with Santa, you have him for a full hour or more. That means more time for photos. More time for Santa to "really" talk with your children. And, more time to get photos with everyone, even Aunt Harriett or Grandma.

The same goes for having Santa come to a business or community event. Again, Santa will have more time to give that personal visit with the children and you will have more time to take lots of photos.

There are lots of ways to find a Santa. Depending on the age of the audience, you can have a friend or neighbor put on a beard and wig, and the famous "red suit."

If your Santa is for an all adult party, such as an association or company event, anyone could be your Santa. The important thing here is celebrating Santa's visit and getting those fun photos to post on Facebook and Instagram.

When the event is with toddlers and preschoolers, who own the most creative imaginations, just about anyone can be their Santa. Whether the person in the red suit is a young person or old, man or woman, a small child's view will be clouded with the magic their mind creates. They will see the person in front of them as the "real" Santa Claus.

However, when the children get beyond pre-school age, into first grade and beyond, the imagination is reduced and more logic and truth develops. As they get older, they begin to see more detail and often can spot someone wearing a beard or wig.

This change has prompted the need for more realism and the evolution of the "Real Bearded" Santa Claus. Just about every Mall and Shopping Center today, demands that the Santa on their holiday set, is "real bearded."

So, if the children at your party are in this category, you too should consider hiring a 'real bearded" Santa.

There are a lot of companies that offer this type of Santa.

www.RealSantas.com is one of those companies that can supply a real bearded Santa for a home or personal visit.

Now, I must be honest, this is my company. It is one of the nation's largest listings of Real Bearded Santas in every state and region, and have supplied Santa to Coca-Cola, Macy's, Microsoft, Amazon, Sam's Club, Sears, Wal-Mart and many more.

You can also search the web for a local agency that offers entertainment.

* * * * * * * *

To help you in making Santa's visit a most enjoyable event, we have prepared the following list of suggestions.

1.   **Have your camera/s ready**.   Be sure to have all the video cards, thumb drives, film, videotape and batteries necessary to take the photos you want or need to get.   And don't forget to make sure there is room on your phone for all those photos and selfies.

2.   **Reserve a special parking place for Santa**.   It should be as close as possible to where he is visiting.   Santa is a senior citizen and needs to park directly in front or next to the house, or business, or party location.   He cannot park down the street or in a parking garage & hike to your location.   He will be winded or exhausted, when he gets there.

If at a home, a car could back down the driveway a little, leaving a space in front of the car.   When Santa arrives, the host could pull the car up and Santa parks behind it.   Or, put a temporary barrier in the space reserved for Santa.   Use a box, a chair or a sawhorse.   Have some fun; put a sign out "Reserved for Santa!"   If your event is at a business or a company facility, office building or hotel, try to decide for Santa to park in a valet or loading area.

You should also have someone designated to meet and guide Santa to the event.

This makes it easier for him to be fresh and ready to bring joy to your guests.

3.   **Meet Santa when he arrives**: to assist him.   The host or someone can show him where to park; to help load any presents into his special "Santa" bag; and to escort him to the location of the event.   If there is a balance or payment due to Santa, place it inside a Christmas card or

envelope.　Never give Santa money in front of the Children.　It can ruin the magic of the moment.　The host or coordinator meeting Santa outside should take care of any final payments that are due before Santa enters.

4.　**Have your gifts ready.**　Santa normally does not bring any candy canes or gifts with him.　He will hand out your candy and gifts and can carry in one bag of presents for children or guests, about 40 pounds.　Presents should be well labeled. We suggest a large black marking pen and writing directly on the gift, as tags can easily fall off.　All packages should fit into one 35-gallon trash bag.　He will transfer the gifts to his "official" Santa Bag.

If you have more than one bag, check with Santa and see if there is a way to have the gifts near his chair before he arrives or if there is a way for you to have "helpers" bring the extra gifts in, after he enters.

5.　**Get everyone together, before Santa enters**. Timing is everything.　You have scheduled Santa for a set amount of time, which begins the minute he arrives. Unless otherwise arranged, he will not be able to stay longer than he has been booked for.　If everyone is scattered around the house or office, you lose valuable time.　Santa and you can coordinate.　He should call you when he is five minutes away from arriving. That's your cue to get everyone together, maybe to sing some Christmas Carols, and to have someone go outside to meet Santa.

Then, at the right moment the host enters and gets all the children singing "Jingle Bells!"　Santa will then pop-in and joins everyone in their singing.　If you have a large group of children to see Santa, you should assign someone to be Santa's helper, and to hand him the presents.

6.   **Have a sturdy chair for Santa to sit in**. Folding chairs and low chairs (the one's you sink into) are not good. Santa usually likes a chair that is sturdy and stable. A good straight-back dining chair, with no arms, works well. He should be able to sit comfortably, and the chair needs to support him plus a child on each knee.

7.   **Place the Chair near your Christmas tree**. Or in a holiday setting. Your photos will have more impact when the background has a festive look. Place a wreath, a few Christmas cards or your children's drawings on the wall to make a wonderful difference. Leave a foot or two between the chair and the tree or wall. This will allow room for others to gather around and behind Santa's chair for group photos. Fireplaces do look nice but remember putting Santa too close to a real fire is not good for his comfort or health!

8.   **Think about photos with everyone**. Yes, some teenagers might think it is too childish, to have a photo with Santa. Don't worry; Santa can stand up for a "buddy" photo. What about grandma and grandpa? Take a photo with Santa and Grandma Hugging. And Santa can take group photos with all the ladies or a "Team" photo with the guys. And yes! Santa loves "Selfies!" More photos of Santa show up on Facebook© and Instagram© than almost any other celebrity."

©2003, 2005, 2008 & 2017 Timothy Connaghan

21 FIGHTING THE BIG "D"

Possibly the greatest obstacle to enjoying the holidays is the gloom and depression that seems to arrive with the Fall and Winter months.

Holiday Depression. That is one of the major reasons I wrote this book.

I hear thousands of wishes every year. Mostly from children. But sometimes from adults. Sometimes their wish is to get rid of the stress and depression.

If this Santa could grant one wish, it might be to eliminate and reduce holiday depression.

Unfortunately, my answer to any such requests, is, "Santa's Magic is Toys."

Each of us needs to understand, that we are always going to have some forms of stress. If we do not understand, or know how to handle our stress, we can get bogged down and even develop bits of depression.

Most of the chapters in this book cover things you can do to handle the added pressures of the holidays. By starting your planning a few months earlier and being a bit more organized, you will have less stress during the holiday season.

However, before you start reading about creating your holiday plan, and if you will allow me, I would like to offer my thoughts regarding the whys and ways that one can get depressed at holiday times. I believe that knowing and understanding, often helps in working through any problem.

WHERE DOES HOLIDAY STRESS COME FROM

Well, to start, let us assume that you have your regular daily activities and/or work. Does any of your daily routine have a stress level? Or, are you stress-free?

Most of us have a normal amount of stress in our day-to-day activities. But what happens when things change?

It is said that some of our fall and winter stress may come with the change of seasons and the fact that we are losing sunlight and gaining darkness.

This annual change of seasons may conversely bring on certain changes in moods and feelings.

Some studies have proven as the overcast and darkness of late Fall and Winter arrive, and our daylight gets shorter, an aura of gloom can affect how we live and work.

These darkening changes affect our going to work or school in the now darker morning and returning home in the gray and dark afternoon hours. And if you are driving during these times, it is even more stressful.

So now everyone must add these changes to their daily routine. How do you handle it?

Each of us in our own way, often counters our gloom by changing our daily routine. Many have found that having brighter lighting in the home and office during these months helps to reduce the gloom.

Unfortunately, no matter what some of us do, this seasonal gloom can increase levels of daily stress.

Can you can see how levels of stress can increase? Can we all agree, when most of us arrive at this time of year, we may have just a 'little' stress?

The seasonal reduction of daylight is just one possible factor to stress. Here are a few other contributors:

- In the work place, many employers assume that summer vacations and fun are over. They seem to tighten operations and demand more production. So naturally they want everyone to work a bit harder. Yes, employers might contribute to our stress.

- If you are a parent, the kids are going back to school! And for some parents there are more responsibilities to help the kids do homework, school projects and, meet with the teachers on those all-important parent-teacher nights. Again, this can add to our stress.

- And there is more. To this we can add the Fall events and celebrations, Halloween and Thanksgiving, plus any parties, socials, family events or dinners that are associated with them.

- But wait, there is even more! Finally, there is the biggest holiday month of all, December, with its shopping, cooking, events and gift giving. No wonder we sometimes have too much to do and not enough time.

Combined, all of this leads to various forms of stress. It happens to all of us. Sometimes it creates feelings of anxiety.

And sometimes it leads to holiday depression. Or, as I call it the "Big D."

HOLIDAY DEPRESSION CAN IMPACT YOUR LIFE

Holiday depression can build a wall between you and those things you like. And it not only affects you, it can carry over or impact other family members, or fellow workers and those around you.

Have you ever heard a friend refer to someone else as having, "a dark cloud following them?" Sometimes that suggestion is quite easy to believe.

These factors, I just presented, are just some of the contributors to gloom, stress and depression. You may have other contributors.

I am not a professional, I can't really consult or advise you, on what to do. Only you know your situation and only you are the one who must act.

And even if it is not you who is depressed, but possibly it's a friend or family member, hopefully you can step in and aid or give advice.

No wonder some people get a little depressed. Many folks who stress out during the holidays find they can't seem to get going or can't seem to enjoy anything. So, they often have bouts of depression. Sometimes it is just a bit too much to take in.

Reducing depression can be as simple as talking to someone else, sharing your problem or situation. Just sharing the information can help to lighten the load on your shoulders. And sometimes the clouds disappear, and everything seems much clearer.

Maybe you can talk to a family member or friend. Sharing your problem or concern with someone else, can aid in lightening the burden or stress that affects you.

For some, the depression may be a bit deeper or more compounded. These forms of depression may require counseling or medical assistance. In these cases, one should look to getting assistance or counseling.

Sometimes, you can consult with a doctor, clergyman, or other professional for help. They can give us advice on how to get out from under those dark clouds.

STRESS CAN AFFECT EVERYONE

Surprisingly stress can touch everyone. From the oldest adult to the youngest child. I know for most of those reading this book, it is personal and usually what adults experience.

But I thought you might like to know that stress can affect everyone. So before going onto how stress affect adults, let me tell you about some of the children

Often, when appearing as Santa, I will be with a child who wants to tell me their holiday wishes or requests. But instead of a toy, or game or the average gift request, they bring a wish for something that is difficult to grant.

They share with Santa, their most personal wishes. Often social in nature and intangible, these are the deepest worries a child can have. And although they do not know it, these children are stressed.

"Can Santa stop my Mom and Dad from getting a divorce?" Or, "Can you help my parents get back together?"

Sometimes it is a child's wish to bring a parent home from deployment in the military. And sometimes it is asking Santa to cure someone of a serious illness.

Unfortunately, Santa often cannot grant wishes for intangible things. As I said earlier, "Santas Magic is Toys."

The children's difficult wishes or requests are something that Santa has no control over and cannot grant.

And yet, there is a way for Santa to give some form of answer that will appease the child and hopefully reduce their worry and stress.

In each of the above instances the child is worried and often has some form of depression. Often the child will take on the idea that they could be a part of the problem.

As Santa, I must first acknowledge to the child that I heard what they said. I must, in some way, compassionately let them know it is something I have no control over. But, I then remind them that they are loved by their parents, or loved ones, and that Santa loves them too!

Then it is time to move on, changing the subject, and helping the child to decide what they want on Christmas morning.

Now, hopefully, as that child is leaving Santa, they will feel a bit better because they shared their problem. And possibly Santa has helped reduce the stress and any depression that might have been there.

I have used the above story about children with stress to give you an example. It's about sharing a problem. Sometimes when you share, the worry is diminished, and your load can be lightened.

Lightening your load – Reducing Stress

Speaking of lightening your load, if you see something that looks too big to tackle, and you keep putting it off, may I suggest you try to break it down into smaller tasks and possibly do one task at a time.

And don't keep your problems bottled up. It only adds to more stress and can agitate or stir up the depression.

Sometimes we find our own ways to get around it. You can check out the internet for information and assistance. Or read one or more of self-help books that are out there.

In this way you can learn about the causes of stress or depression, and hopefully find advice, solutions and aids that will help you eliminate Stress and fight Depression.

There are also some excellent motivational recordings and CD's, that you can listen to or play while driving.

You may learn that it can be as simple as using brighter lights in the home. It could be joining a Yoga or Tai Chi class. Or it could be getting a little more organization in your life. It's up to you.

I think Depression can, and does, touch all of us at some time in our life. Often it is something short lived.

Some experts have written that depression and stress usually follow emotional events. Everything from a big birthday, to a wedding to a funeral. They are all big emotional events.

Most Holiday Professionals, I included, have heavy workloads and burdens in November and December. Often, Santa, the elves, photographers, and party planners are very busy for weeks on end, helping at events that bring joy and happiness to others.

And what the average person does not know, is that most Holiday professionals are often behind in their own holiday shopping, decorating, and often they miss the joy of being with their own families.

So, Santas get stressed, too!

If the "Big D" and stress are getting in your way, you need to work on eliminating them, or at least controlling them.

I original started writing this book as a simple, 3-page, checklist for many of the holiday professionals I work with.

In sharing the checklists with others, I received many comments and suggestions. And from my fellow professionals, I realized that there was more needed than just a check list. That led to more research and creating this book!

22 THE MAGIC OF THE HOLIDAYS

Every family has its own heritage, culture, and beliefs. It is one of the wonderful elements of life that we can experience and enjoy.

As god has made us, we know that in many ways, we are alike. Yet, none of us is exactly like anyone else.

The same goes with families. A lot of families mirror or do the same things as other families do. However, as we are all different, so too is every family different from another family.

The similarities we share help to bring us all together. And the differences give us variety, present new experiences and create new insight into our world.

From cultural and historical differences to the legendary and fantasy that artists have given us, we have many things to enjoy during the holidays.

Hopefully the tools and ideas presented in this book will give you more time to enjoy the holidays and to expand the experiences of the most wonderful time of the year.

The holiday season is filled with so much magic. Much of it is the wonderful decorations and events that go with the holidays. And whether it is from a department store, or your neighbors or fiends, it is there to enjoy.

But there is so much more magic. It is what we experience through our children. It is their excitement when they meet Santa. Or when they open a gift. It's the joy they get when lighting a candle on the Menorah.

And so often we are blessed to see and feel their joy. It is something we really cannot touch. Yet we can feel it and enjoy the warmth and joy it can bring.

The same goes when we see a child opening that present, that says, 'From Santa,' but is really from us. Again, we can feel the warmth and excitement as the child rips away the wrapping and finds that their wish has been granted.

And even if you do not have a child in your home or can view someone opening a gift from you, I invite you to consider bringing some magic to someone less fortunate.

Donating your time to a charity or donating to Toys for Tots or one of the other charities that offer aid at Christmas is truly one of the ways we can extend the spirit of giving and truly enjoy the Magic of the Holidays.

ADDENDUM

Now that you some of the ways to "Get a Head Start and Survive the Holidays," you can automatically be the recipient of a special gift.

By "Getting Ahead," your gift is extra free time! Time you can use as you please. Time to relax. Time to spend on yourself. Or, time to do something special. Here are a few suggestions for using your new free time:

- Schedule time at the beginning of the month to make phone calls to relatives and old friends. Call someone who would never expect it.

  Call someone who cannot get out to visit. Call a child and pretend you are Santa or Mrs. Claus. Make one or two calls a day if you can. You will be surprised how much energy you will get from making these calls.

- Take a gift to someone who would not expect it. Nothing beats the warm fuzzy feeling you get when doing a "Random Act of Kindness."

I never need the services of a crossing guard, but there is one local crossing guard near my home that works extremely hard. I see her once or twice a week and we exchange smiles. And she always has a smile, for everyone walking or driving by. Last year I made a quick stop and gave the crossing guard some fresh baked cookies. She didn't know my name and I didn't know hers. But I really felt great after giving him that tin of cookies.

- Maybe you have a friend or neighbor who cannot get out. Offer to take them shopping or to do their shopping for them. Address some Christmas cards for them.

  Bring some holiday cheer into their life! If you have children, invite them to help wrap the gifts or mail the cards. Get the family involved. It's the true Spirit of Christmas.

- Finally, always remember, no matter what you have on your calendar, schedule time for yourself and your family. Write down appointments to stay home and do things together.

  Schedule time when you and the family can just sit around and watch an old movie or better yet to make some cookies or put together some little gift baskets to give as those surprise gifts.

Take advantage of your gift of time, for when it is gone, it's gone forever.

ADDENDUM

ACTIVITY PLANNING GUIDE

The following five pages are your planning guide form. You can make copies and use them for any type of project or planning. Or you can download the complete form as 1) a word document that you can edit, or 2) as a PDF form to fill out by hand.

Downloads at: http://www.nationalsanta.com/project-or-task-planning-guide/

---

1. What is the primary activity or task you wish to accomplish? This is a mini description of what task or activity you need to work on. It gives a focus to what you want to do.

_____

_____

_____

_____

_____

_____

_____

2. What are the specific goals to be accomplished? Here is where you start getting into details. How many people will be involved? Are there costs? List what elements or things that will be completed. (Use numbers if that will help)

_____

_____

_____

_____

_____

_____

_____

3. What are the specific manpower assignments? Make a list of jobs, duties, tasks, and assignments. Is this something you will do yourself or will you have other family members assist. Or maybe you will hire or have someone else do the task. (Put names with each task) (If you have phone numbers, list those too.)

_____

_____

_____

_____

4. What materials and supplies will you need for this activity? Think about or walk through the actual task you are working on. If it is in a special location, why not be there. If you can't do that, imagine you are there. Think about how you will be set up? What will be going on? If others are with you, what is everyone doing? As you imagine the activity, list what materials and supplies you will need. Create a list or checklist to help yourself and anyone working with you. Review the lists in your planning. It will aid you in shopping and making sure nothing   is   forgotten.

_____

_____

_____

_____

_____

_____

_____

_____

_____

5. What outside resources will be used? These are items someone else will supply or bring. These may be items from the last question. It could also be what a vendor, contractor or caterer is responsible for. List the items, supplies, materials, and or equipment they are responsible for. This is especially true if what you need is not normally at your home or the location of the activity. Review your checklist and single out items you might be able to borrow or have someone else bring.

_____

_____

_____

_____

_____

_____

_____

6. What problems do you worry about, or anticipate needing to overcome, to successfully complete this activity?

This is sometimes call negative brainstorming. Think of all the things that could interfere or go wrong with this activity. Decide on how you might take care of the problem if it arises. Can you fix it? Will you need to cancel it? Have a simple plan on how you plan to address the problem. Once you have a plan, you can move on to the next   activity.

_____

_____

_____

_____

_____

_____

_____

7.   List the specific steps to be taken. This is your time line for this activity. What steps do you need to make or take to bring this activity to a successful competition? Sometimes you can make a task simpler by breaking down the work into smaller tasks, and then spreading them out. Create a time line.

_____

_____

_____

_____

_____

_____

_____

_____

_____

_____

_____

_____

8. What are your costs. If there are costs, say for the materials and supplies you need, list them here. If you need to buy something, add it here. These items need to be in your budget. Think of food for meals: boxes, paper and gift wrap; gifts to order, decorations; postage and shipping, fees or payments carpet cleaning or to vendors, etc. Even cash gifts or donations you might want to make. Knowing the costs of an activity may also be a factor in deciding to go through with it or cancel it.

_____

_____

_____

_____

_____

_____

_____

_____

SANTA'S HANDY HINTS

Here are some extra hints and suggestions that I would like to offer:

1. Use your computer, Tablet or phone to search for deals. This is my #1 Handy Hint.

    a. Today's retailers all have web sites and just about any product you are thinking about can be found on the internet. No matter what search engine you use, you can enter the store or key words or the name of for the item you think Aunt Harriet will like, and "voila," it will probably appear.

    b. Using the internet also allows you to do comparison shopping, as often you can find the same or similar items at lower prices.

    c. Don't forget to use those magic search words, "coupon," and "sale," and you will also get info on any special offers, etc.

    d. The internet is also very valuable as many times you can find products that are not available in the store but are available on-line. This is very true with Cosco, Sam's, Target and many large retailers.

Often products that are not popular sale items for your region are not in the local store. So

e.   Use the internet to find other web sites that offer handy hints for holiday shopping. Often you can get great advice on when to shop for food stuffs, when the best days are for buying electronics, etc.

2.   Some of these web sites even offer notification services for specials that come up on line. This is not for everyone, as lots of us don't want too many emails and texts. But, when amid holiday shopping, you might want some help.

3.   Double check with your retailer for "free shipping," and "free gift-wrapping." These two items along can save you both money and time.

a.   And if you are shipping, check to see if they can designate the day or delivery. If not, be sure the delivery is at least early. Better early than too late.

b.   Some delivery's with UPS, FED-EX and even the USPS all have tracking, and you can get updates on when an item will be delivered, has been delivered, etc. You can even get updates sent to your phone, tablet or computer!

4.   Only buy or purchase from well-known on-line retailers. Or if purchasing via eBay, make sure you have buyer protection.

a.   Avoid getting swindled. Never send cash or money orders. I recommend you use a major credit card with some form of buyer protection.

5.   Use your lists to make sure you don't miss anyone.

6. Avoid impulse buying. One of the biggest mistakes made at the holidays, is over-buying, or impulse buying. Even if a sign says "Sale," it may not always be a good bargain.

7. Make sure you get gift receipts for those gifts that might need to be returned. And be sure to know the stores return policies.

8. Don't assume that all gifts are returnable. Many of today's retailers have complicated return policies or make you go through so many hoops, they hope you will give up.

9. Start early with your shopping. Whether it is gifts for the family or food stuffs for those special meals and baking, it is never too early to stop shopping and stocking up.

a. Many folks set up special shelves in the pantry for their holiday foods. Some even clear a little space in the freezer so when they see a special item on sale early, they can take advantage of the lower prices and freeze the item until the holidays.

b. The same goes for a special shelf or even a closet where you can start collecting your gifts, prior to wrapping them.

10. As the holidays approach, stores will begin having special displays with holiday food stuffs and baking items. Be ready for these special sales and stock up early.

26 ABOUT THE AUTHOR

"National Santa™" - Timothy Connaghan

In case you were wondering who the world's busiest and most active Santa is, look no further than National Santa™ Tim Connaghan!

- Media and Marketing Event Santa for Coca-Cola, K-Mart, Amazon, and dozens of national campaigns and television specials
- Santa in commercials for Oreo, Sears, Target, Dannon, Swisscom, Ritz, Cool Whip, Planters, & More
- National Santa for the Marine Corps Reserve Toys for Tots Foundation
- Official Santa for the Hollywood Christmas Parade – America's Premiere Celebrity Santa
- Producer of "Discover Santa 2016" the World's largest Santa Convention.
- One of America's foremost experts on Santa Claus & the Business of Santa.
- Author – "Behind the Red Suit – the Business of Santa" – America's #1 Santa Training Book
- Author – "Surviving the Holidays"

- 2011 Inductee – Santa Claus Hall of Fame.

- 2013 Honoree - Charles W. Howard Award.

- Graduated over 4,000 Santas & Mrs. Claus from his International University of Santa Claus, aka: School4Santas!

- Owner of America's largest Santa Booking agency RealSantas.com

- Founding President to one of America's Largest Santa Groups.

Hand-picked by Hollywood's Original Honorary Mayor, Johnny Grant, Connaghan is now celebrating 50 years of wearing the Red Suit, & his fifteenth year as the **Official Santa for the Hollywood Christmas Parade**.

He also serves as the National Santa for the **Marine Corps Reserve Toys for Tots**, assisting with nation promotions and humanitarian toy deliveries during major disasters. For the past five years he has had the honor of joining with the Marines at the **NYSE**, for the opening or closing bell ceremonies on Black Friday

Many honors have been presented to Santa Tim, but the most prestigious is his induction by the Santa Claus Oath Foundation, into the **International Santa Claus Hall of Fame** at Santa Claus, Indiana in December of 2011.

Santa Tim has been seen by millions on Dr. Phil, The Today Show, Tonight Show, The Doctors, CBS This Morning, Rikki Lake, Fox

and Friends, & Ryan Seacrest Show. He has acted in movies & television shows, including: "Castle," "It's Complicated," "Southland," "Suburgatory," "Cinema Vérité" and "The Mentalist."

He has also appeared on five

catalogue covers for J.C. Penney, and in commercials for Oreos, CBS, Target, Sears, Old Navy, Honey baked ham, Dannon, and Swiss-Com.

His clients include Amazon, Coca-Cola, Disney, Microsoft, Southwest Airlines, Radio City Music Hall, Macy's, Hershey's, Toys R Us, K-Mart, Hallmark, I-Hop, In-N-Out Burgers, Branson CVB, McDonalds, Hertz, Wal-Mart & Sam's Clubs and Warner Bros.

As an Entrepreneur & entertainer he has established himself in the Santa world, through his personal contributions, and as President of **The Kringle Group**, which includes a variety of business activities,

Through his **School4Santas**, recognized as the largest annual Professional Santa School in the world & officially known as the **International University of Santa Claus**, (IUSC), he has awarded diplomas to over 4,000 Santas & Mrs. Claus.

A "24/7/365" Santa, he also directs **RealSantas.com**, one of the world's busiest Holiday suppliers of Santas for malls, photo studios & special events all over the world, & supplying 'real beard' Santas for as many as 1,400 events & promotions each year.

Santa Tim's annual release of Santa Statistics & his position in the Santa community are well known & have led to appearances on all network news channels. the Neil Cavuto Show, CNN, NBC, ABC's Nightline, Bloomberg News, Fox News & PBS, plus interviews in Time, the Wall Street Journal, Reader's Digest, Los Angeles Times, & hundreds of local, regional, national & international media. (Art sketch c/o Wall Street Journal)

Tim Connaghan

A major figure at spectacular events, nationally televised tree lightings and parades, & celebrity parties, including The Kodak Theater, The Grove in Los Angeles, Knott's Berry Farm, Hollywood & Highland, Capitol Records, Los Angeles Country Club, Riviera Country Club, Blue Bloods, The USO, Dr. Phil & Robin McGraw, Reese Witherspoon,

James Iovine, Candy Spelling, Joel Silver, Marvin & Barbara Davis & Steven Spielberg.

For three years, he directed one of the world's largest Santa associations serving as the founding president for AORBS, the Amalgamated Order of Real Bearded Santas, where, in 2006, produced **"Discover Santa,"** the first modern day Santa Claus Convention with over 500 Santas and Mrs. Claus and world-wide media coverage including all television networks and a feature article in Time Magazine.

Recently, in July of 2016, he directed **"Discover Santa 2016,"** the tenth anniversary convention attended by over 1,000 Santas and Mrs. Claus.

A native Californian & the oldest of eleven children, Tim's first experience as Santa occurred on December 23, 1969. Wearing a beard of Barbasol shaving cream he handed out holiday packages to his fellow soldiers serving in Viet Nam.

He served in the U.S. Army's 9th Infantry Division & is a recipient of the Bronze Star & other awards. In February 2008, he was awarded the Military Legion of Honor's Humanitarian Award.

Upon his return home, he attended Long Beach City College & California State University at Long Beach where he majored in Communications. In addition, he holds certificates in Corporate Communications and Fundraising from USC (University of Southern California).

❄ ❄ ❄ ❄ ❄ ❄

Made in the USA
Middletown, DE
31 December 2018